UNDERSTANDING
ISLAM

BY GAIL RADLEY

CONTENT CONSULTANT

Sana Tayyen

Visiting Scholar
School of Religion
University of Southern California
Visiting Assistant Professor
University of Redlands

Essential Library

An Imprint of Abdo Publishing | abdopublishing.com

UNDERSTANDING WORLD RELIGIONS AND BELIEFS

ABDOPUBLISHING.COM

Published by Abdo Publishing, a division of ABDO, PO Box 398166, Minneapolis, Minnesota 55439. Copyright © 2019 by Abdo Consulting Group, Inc. International copyrights reserved in all countries. No part of this book may be reproduced in any form without written permission from the publisher. Essential Library™ is a trademark and logo of Abdo Publishing.

Printed in the United States of America, North Mankato, Minnesota
042018
092018

THIS BOOK CONTAINS RECYCLED MATERIALS

Cover Photo: Shutterstock Images
Interior Photos: Achmad Ibrahim/AP Images, 4–5; Patrick T. Fallon/Reuters/Newscom, 8–9; Lai Seng Sin/AP Images, 11; Khalid Tanveer/AP Images, 12; Ray Ellis/Science Source, 14–15; iStockphoto, 17, 36; Rainer Lesniewski/Shutterstock Images, 23; F. G. Mayer/Science Source, 26–27; Pictures From History/Newscom, 29, 46; Nico Tondini Danita Delimont Photography/Newscom, 33; Lefteris Pitarakis/AP Images, 40; Leo Lin Tang/Shutterstock Images, 42–43; Heri Juanda/AP Images, 48–49; Kamran Jebreili/AP Images, 52–53; Stefano Florentino/iStockphoto, 54–55; Nick Ut/AP Images, 58–59; Richard Drew/AP Images, 63; AP Images, 65; Hubert Boesl/picture-alliance/dpa/AP Images, 66–67; Karim Kadim/AP Images, 72–73; World History Archive/Newscom, 76; Chris Huby/Le Pictorium/Newscom, 79; John Stillwell/PA Images/Getty Images, 81; Taras Studio/Shutterstock Images, 84 (top left); Shutterstock Images, 84 (top right); IPG GutenbergUK Ltd/iStockphoto, 84 (bottom left); Don Bartletti/Los Angeles Times/Getty Images, 84 (bottom right); Jacquelyn Martin/AP Images, 86; Nagel Photography/Shutterstock Images, 88–89; Red Line Editorial, 92; Vincent Thian/AP Images, 94; Laura Leon/AP Images, 97

Editor: Marie Pearson
Series Designer: Maggie Villaume

LIBRARY OF CONGRESS CONTROL NUMBER: 2017961411

PUBLISHER'S CATALOGING-IN-PUBLICATION DATA

Name: Radley, Gail, author.
Title: Understanding Islam / by Gail Radley.
Description: Minneapolis, Minnesota : Abdo Publishing, 2019. | Series: Understanding world religions and beliefs | Includes online resources and index.
Identifiers: ISBN 9781532114267 (lib.bdg.) | ISBN 9781532154096 (ebook)
Subjects: LCSH: Islam--Doctrines--Juvenile literature. | Islam and culture--Juvenile literature. | World religions--Juvenile literature. | Religious belief--Juvenile literature.
Classification: DDC 297.0--dc23

CONTENTS

FASTING AND FEASTING

In Indonesia, home of the world's largest Muslim population, children marched the streets in costume, carrying torches to announce the coming of Ramadan. When Muslims in India spotted the crescent moon, signaling the arrival of a new month, broadcasters across the country announced that Ramadan was beginning. In the United States, the faithful gathered in mosques for prayers that evening. They began fasting the next day, eating nothing between their predawn breakfasts and their postsunset meals.

Ramadan is the ninth month of the Islamic calendar. This calendar is lunar, following the cycles of the moon. It is shorter than the solar Gregorian calendar used in the United States because the lunar cycle is a little shorter than a Gregorian month. So Ramadan happens in all of the seasons over time. The month honors the time when the Prophet Muhammad received his first revelation from God.

Many Indonesian Muslim children participate in the Ramadan torch parade.

Muhammad lived in what is now Saudi Arabia from 570 to 632 CE. He recorded God's revelations in the Islamic holy book, the Koran.

YOUNG PEOPLE ON RAMADAN

An online news site based in Dubai, a city in the United Arab Emirates, asked young people what Ramadan meant to them. Reem Al Mannaei, age nine, said, "I was very happy I was able to participate in the Holy Month with my family and friends. Though it was a bit difficult in school as we had to concentrate on studies too." New to Dubai, 17-year-old Margaret Cowart added, "I feel it is a beautiful time when Muslims reflect, believe and worship Allah. The Holy Month of Ramadan not only teaches Muslims to learn patience, humility and spirituality through fasting, but will also help me become more culturally aware and respectful."[1]

In addition to fasting during Ramadan, Muslims remember to give to charity, especially during the month's last days. They typically eat dates, with their sugary bursts of energy, at the end of a day's fast, followed by a sip of water. Ramadan is a practice of detachment from worldly things, a time to focus on living a spiritual life. It also provides a reminder of people in poverty, for whom fasting may not be a choice.

Some Muslim children work their way toward the full fast by avoiding food and drink a few hours each day. But most don't begin until puberty. Children aren't required to fast, nor are the sick, the elderly, or pregnant or nursing mothers, but many are eager to participate in this sacred time.

ISLAMIC HOLY DAYS

For most Muslims, there are only two festivals, Eid al-Fitr and Eid al-Adha. Although the dates of these festivals change on the Gregorian calendar, they are the same days on the Islamic calendar each year. Eid al-Adha celebrates the time when Abraham agreed to sacrifice his son, Ishmael, at God's request. Abraham is known as Ibrahim in Arabic, and Ishmael is Isma'il. In the end, God allows Abraham to sacrifice a sheep instead. For Muslims, this event is a reminder to submit to God in whatever he requires. The holiday is typically celebrated by sacrificing an animal and sharing the meat among family, friends, and the poor. People say prayers and give presents.

Muslims debate additional holidays, as some feel no holidays should be added to those the Prophet mentioned, not even his birthday. Some do celebrate his birthday, however, usually by recalling his life and giving to charity. The Islamic New Year remembers Muhammad's journey from Mecca to Medina to escape persecution. Some Muslims observe the New Year by fasting, praying, reflecting, and even holding parades.

Islam uses a lunar, or moon-based, calendar, so the dates of these observances change yearly on the Gregorian calendar. The day ends and the new one begins at sunset. A holiday on May 3 would begin at sunset on May 2.

Eid al-Fitr

All Muslims, however, observe Eid al-Fitr, the festival of breaking the fast, which lasts three days. After the long month of contemplation and self-control, more than one billion Muslims worldwide rejoice at seeing a sliver of the new moon appear, starting off the new month with this joyous holiday. Everyone who is able wears new clothes; children often receive money and other presents for the occasion, too. The first day typically begins with prayers at a large mosque or other hall. Some pray outdoors. In

Anaheim, California, for example, 20,000 believers arrived at
Angel Stadium to launch the June 2017 Eid festivities.[2]

Some might imagine the Anaheim event as drawing
together only Middle Easterners, reflecting the faith's origins.
But at Angel Stadium, attendees of all races gathered. "You
see people of all races and many cultures here, but we're all
Americans," said attorney Omar Siddiqui, adding, "Most of us
were born here."[3]

In Egypt, Saudi Arabia, and other Muslim-majority
countries, Eid al-Fitr is a national holiday. Believers gather in
large or central mosques. Some travel to a holy city, such as
Mecca in Saudi Arabia, for prayers. Hundreds of thousands
pray in the early morning at the Great Mosque of Mecca. The
Imam, or prayer leader, will call "Allahu Akbar!" meaning "God
is great!" in Arabic.[4] Worshippers tell each other, "Eid Mubarak,"
Arabic for "Blessed Eid."[5]

Because food marks the end of fasting, it is an important
part of the festivities. While recipes differ according to personal

EID AL-FITR BREAKFAST

While it is common to break fast with a date, the Eid al-Fitr breakfast often continues with some other special breakfast treats. Muslims in India, Pakistan, and Bangladesh like to start the day with *sheer khurma*, in which vermicelli noodles are made into a soup-like pudding with milk. Moroccans are likely to choose buttered couscous, called *laasida*. In Iraq, a favorite choice is bread and honey with buffalo cream, a thick, rich cream that comes from a buffalo's milk.

preference, culture, and available ingredients, traditionally, believers offer cake or other sweets to friends and family. Some go into the streets to include strangers. One Palestinian Muslim woman makes up to 600 little cakes for this purpose.[6] Although she isn't always able to make so many, she does what she can to continue the tradition. Some Muslims make *ma'amoul*, or date cakes, to share with others. Muslims in Bangladesh eat spicy rice with chicken or another meat. In India, soldiers offer treats to passersby. Muslims who have moved to Western countries can usually find the ingredients for their family's traditional foods at ethnic markets, or they may enjoy their favorite Western foods. Eid traditions vary with the culture, but they often include festivals and big meals with family and friends. Women often decorate their hands in beautiful henna designs.

Muslims make or buy sweets to serve for Eid al-Fitr.

Muslim women use henna to make beautiful designs in celebration of Eid al-Fitr.

A Major World Religion

Muslims are followers of Muhammad, who taught that there is but one God, the same God that Jews and Christians believe in. Muslims call him Allah, which is simply Arabic for "God." Muhammad's teachings and guidance for living are contained in a book called the Koran, which Muslims believe was dictated to him by the angel Gabriel.

Muslims are the people who follow the religion Islam. Islam is the world's fastest-growing religion and the second largest, following Christianity. In 2015, the Pew Research Center noted that if it continues to grow at its current rate, Islam will be the world's largest religion by the end of the century.

HENNA FOR HANDS AND FEET

Henna is a dye made from the flowering henna shrub's leaves. Grinding these leaves into a powder to create temporary decorations is popular today. Henna was used in ancient Egypt as a perfume and dye. Muslims use henna in various celebrations, including weddings, with the belief that it offers purity and protection to the bride. Different cultures create unique henna designs for brides with different meanings, including health and fertility.

Rarely, people may have allergic reactions to henna. Black henna, which can contain harsh ingredients and may not even use the henna plant, can irritate and even scar the skin. Some medicines contain henna. Cosmetics, hair dye, and hair care products also sometimes contain henna.

THE PROPHET MUHAMMAD

Life was difficult in Arabia during the 500s CE. The area, the birthplace of Islam, is now known as the nation of Saudi Arabia. Largely a desert region, ancient Arabia's towns developed around oases, where people lived primarily through agriculture. Others formed tribes of nomads, trading as they moved from place to place. No matter how people lived, though, belonging to a clan and tribe meant safety and survival. A clan was a group of related families. Several clans banded together to form a tribe. People's honor and social standing were determined by the wealth and influence of the clan and tribe to which they belonged. Tribes often battled each other. Bearing arms against an enemy tribe was a mark of manhood. Weak tribes sought protection from more powerful tribes. Tribes with common enemies sometimes battled together. The death of a

Even today, villages in Saudi Arabia tend to be built near oases.

15

tribesman demanded a death in return or a payment in compensation. Violent disputes could rage on for generations.

Although there were some Jewish and Christian tribes in the area who worshipped a single God, most tribes were polytheists, believers in many gods. Each tribe might have a distinct set of gods it recognized. The tribes did recognize Allah as the supreme God over all others. But they thought little, if at all, of a spiritual meaning to life or an afterlife. Justice was to be carried out in this world and was the tribes' responsibility. Life was especially harsh for the poor, orphans, and women. Sons were a blessing and added to a family's power. However, daughters were often seen as liabilities. One's daughters might end up married to men of lower classes or be raped. Because of these views, daughters were often buried alive at birth or even later. When sons were plentiful, a daughter might also be sacrificed to the gods or killed to limit family size.

At certain times during the year, tribes managed to set aside their hostilities and gather at one of several important shrines. Here, they might settle disputes as they paid homage to stone and wood idols. Families charged with caring for the shrines were highly regarded. The most revered shrine, which sat in the town of Mecca, was the Kaaba, a cube-shaped building with what is believed to be a black meteorite stone in one corner. The building held the various tribes' 360 idols. Generations before Muhammad's birth, his ancestor Qusayy took on custodianship of the Kaaba, and, until Muhammad later took control of it, it was the Quraish tribe's responsibility to care for it and the pilgrims who

People still visit the Kaaba in Mecca today.

visited. This made the Quraish the ruling tribe of Mecca.

A Prophet Is Born

Into this environment Muhammad was born in 570 CE. Despite his tribe's power and prestige, Muhammad received little from these benefits, being from a poor clan within the tribe. His father died before he was born, and his mother followed when he was six years old. What is known about his early life is a combination of history, Islamic belief, and tradition. When his grandfather also died, Muhammad, whose name means "the praised one" in Arabic, went to live with his uncle Abu Talib. Muhammad was approximately eight at this time.

Muhammad was a shepherd as a child. Later, he worked in Mecca's caravan business and helped his uncle in trading goods. Muhammad soon became known not only for his business sense but also for his honesty and his tendency to think deeply. He was often referred to as *al-Amin*, Arabic for "the trustworthy." Not long after his uncle's business began to flounder, Muhammad, then 25, married Khadijah, a wealthy widow whose caravans he managed. Muhammad became his 40-year-old wife's business manager. The couple had six children. Their two sons died in early childhood, but their daughters lived into adulthood. His beloved younger cousin 'Ali lived with them, along with an adopted son, Zayd ibn Harithah, a former slave.

Muhammad went on a retreat one month of each year for contemplation. On one such retreat, in the year 610 CE, when Muhammad was 40, his life changed dramatically. One night, he meditated in a cave on Mount Hira on how the problems he saw around him might be resolved—the mistreatment of women, orphans, and the poor, the misuse of wealth, and others. One account of that night, later referred to as the Night of Power, says that the angel Gabriel appeared. Gabriel gave Muhammad the Arabic command *iqra'*, meaning "read." Muhammad, illiterate, protested that he could not. Then Gabriel held Muhammad tightly, released him, and commanded him again to read. Gabriel commanded him three times, and Muhammad finally cried, "What shall I read?"[1]

Gabriel revealed to him a verse that would become the ninety-sixth chapter of Islam's holy book, the Koran. The word *Koran* means "the recitation" or "discourse" in Arabic. The chapter begins, "Proclaim! In the name of thy Lord and Cherisher, Who created, Created man, out of A clot of congealed blood. Proclaim! And thy Lord is Most Bountiful—He Who taught the pen, Taught man that Which he knew not."[2]

Muhammad fled to his home, looking back to see Gabriel filling the horizon. Terrified, he described to Khadijah what had happened. She then became the first convert to Islam and funded and supported the Islamic message. 'Ali, only nine then, also believed, as did Zayd. After this, the remaining passages of the Koran were revealed to Muhammad over the course of some two decades.

The Early Days of the Faith

Slowly, Muhammad gathered other followers, the first non-family member being Abu Bakr, a merchant. By approximately 613, Muhammad began promoting his message in public. His first messages were simple, but they stirred most people's anger. He had been divinely appointed as Allah's messenger, he said. They should give up idol worship to worship Allah alone and prepare themselves, in thought and action, for Judgment Day. He also spoke out against common practices such as burying female babies, committing injustices to society's weakest, and using unethical business practices.

The end of idol worship was most disturbing to the Meccans. It would mean the end of pilgrimages to Mecca, they feared, and economic ruin. Most of Muhammad's early followers were slaves and young men without position. Against them were all the powers of Mecca. Only his uncle Abu Talib's intervention, spurred by clan loyalty, kept Muhammad from being killed.

On to Medina

Determined to squash this growing religion, the Quraish beat Muhammad's followers, withheld food and drink, and made them suffer the desert heat without protection. Muhammad sent some of his followers who were without family protection to Ethiopia, where the Christian king of Abyssinia welcomed them. Severe trials came to Muhammad in 619. First, Kadijah died, and then his uncle. Without his uncle's protection, he too needed to find safety.

Finally, in 622, Muhammad met and converted several men from Medina to his cause. These men were expecting a new prophet, and they hoped Muhammad would end civil unrest in their city. Ignoring family ties and offending the Meccans, Muhammad sent most of his followers to Medina, which was largely Jewish. Worrying over what Muhammad's next move might be, the Meccans decided to kill him. 'Ali foiled the assassins by

THE NIGHT JOURNEY

According to tradition, in 619, called the Year of Sorrow, Muhammad rode a winged creature called al-Buraq to the seven heavens and the universe's end and entered Allah's presence with the angel Gabriel. Then he went on to Jerusalem, meeting Abraham, Abraham's descendant Moses, Jesus, and others, where he led them in prayers. Next, he and Gabriel climbed a ladder to heaven's Gate of Watchers, again meeting Abraham, Moses, Jesus, and others. Muhammad discussed prayer requirements with Moses, insisting that 50 daily prayers were too burdensome, and the number was reduced to five.[3] A later Shi'ite teacher, Shaykh Ahmad, argued that Muhammad's spirit rather than his physical body traveled.

A HUMBLE PROPHET

While traveling with some followers, Muhammad asked that they prepare goat meat. The goat would have to be killed, skinned, and cooked. Each follower took on a task. When Muhammad said he would gather firewood, they protested, "You are God's Messenger! We will do everything!" Muhammad replied, "I know you would, but that would be discrimination. God does not want his servants to behave as if they were superior to their companions." His followers so revered him that they would gather the water dripping from his arms when he washed his face, considering it blessed. But Muhammad himself prayed for forgiveness 70 times a day.[4]

sleeping in Muhammad's bed while Muhammad and Abu Bakr slipped away to Medina. Realizing Muhammad was gone, they did not harm 'Ali.

Muhammad united the feuding groups in Medina. Whether Muslim, idol worshipper, or Jew, they agreed to defend their community against aggressors and refuse to harbor lawbreakers or those attempting to destroy the peace. All had equal rights. For a while, peace reigned. But some Medinans started resenting Arab leadership and worked against the union Muhammad had formed.

Observing the changes in Medina and Muhammad's influence there, Meccans suspected he might be planning to attack them. In 624, the Meccans attacked Medina in the Battle of Badr. Though outnumbered, Muhammad and his followers defeated them. Several more battles followed, including one in which Mecca won, but its army was too damaged to take the city.

Medina and Mecca, shown on a contemporary map, are approximately 275 miles (443 km) apart by road.

FATIMAH, DAUGHTER OF THE PROPHET

Muhammad and his daughter Fatimah were so close that Muhammad said, "Fatimah is a part of my body; whoever hurts her, has hurt me, and whoever hurts me has hurt God."[5] She often tended to his needs, particularly after her mother's passing in 619. When Meccans stoned Muhammad, Fatimah dressed his wounds; she also tended the wounded on the battlefields. Whenever she entered his mosque, the Prophet rose, demonstrating how to show respect for women.

When she was a young woman, many men longed to marry her. When 'Ali requested this, Muhammad asked his daughter whether she favored the match. She agreed, and Muhammad married them. The couple had two sons.

As Muhammad lay dying, surrounded by family and friends, he whispered something to Fatimah, causing her to cry. Moments later, he whispered again, and she smiled. "I cried because my father told me he did not have much time to live," she explained later. "But then he told me I would follow him soon. I was happy, as I would be with him again."[6] She died a few months after her father.

In 627, 10,000 Meccan warriors tried again to break Muhammad's power. Muhammad could gather only 3,000, but he had a trench built around the city, disrupting the Meccans' plans. Battles and broken truces marred the next few years as Muhammad's enemies were still intent on stopping him. Finally, in 630, Muhammad led a band of soldiers into Mecca, where they met little resistance. A prominent tribal chief pledged his allegiance to Muhammad. Soon many other Meccans followed. Muhammad and 'Ali cleared the Kaaba of its idols, dedicating it to Allah. Then Muhammad returned to Medina, deeming it the center of Islamic politics and spirituality.

The End of an Era

Despite the power and wealth he came to have, Muhammad preferred to live peacefully and simply. He wore plain clothes, ate ordinary food, and kept simple surroundings. "I eat as a slave eats, and sit as a slave sits, for I am a slave (of God)," he explained.[7]

While he could make difficult battle decisions, he ordered his followers to use no more force than required. The battles he fought were with those who were aggressive toward him. When negotiation was possible, he used it. He much preferred being compassionate, gentle, and kind.

In 632, in Medina, Muhammad became ill. He died a few weeks later at age 62 or 63. Muhammad had accomplished much over his lifetime. He united more than 100 different tribes into a single nation, increasing the sense of loyalty and responsibility toward the nation from individuals, families, and tribes. This union naturally invited more freedom of movement, a stronger sense of security, and a greater exchange of ideas and of trade. He also left the Koran, a guide for billions of followers to come.

THE YEARS AFTER THE PROPHET

Shortly after Muhammad's death, a committee of key followers met to choose his successor as leader of Islam. 'Ali and Fatimah, busy with funeral arrangements, were not included. The committee elected Abu Bakr, Muhammad's faithful friend, adviser, and first unrelated believer, to be the caliph, or leader, for life.

However, many signs through the years suggested that Muhammad would have chosen 'Ali. The two men were close. By marrying Muhammad's daughter, 'Ali also became Muhammad's son-in-law. 'Ali was his trusted companion, served him devotedly, and received much praise and honor from the Prophet. At one point, according to Abu Ja'far Muhammad ibn Jarir al-Tabari, whose history of the Prophet is accepted by almost all Muslims, Muhammad

After Muhammad's death, Islam grew and Muslims began conquering many regions.

gathered his clan and, wrapping an arm around 'Ali, announced, "This is my brother, my trustee and my successor among you, so listen to him and obey."[1] While some followers joked that 'Ali's father must now obey his son, some Muslims cite this as evidence of Muhammad's choice. And during Muhammad's last pilgrimage, he took 'Ali's hand, saying, "Of whomsoever I am Lord, then 'Ali is also his Lord. O God! Be Thou the supporter of whoever supports 'Ali and the enemy of whoever opposes him."[2] The Shi'a division of Islam, Arabic for "Party of 'Ali," would later form around the idea that 'Ali should have been Muhammad's first successor, followed by 'Ali's sons, Hasan and Husayn. Muslims belonging to Shi'a are called Shi'ites. Those who believe Abu Bakr was the rightful first caliph are called Sunnis.

Each side believed Muhammad had confirmed its choice of successors prior to his death, citing the Prophet's words in support of their claims. But these words could be interpreted differently. The followers were not able to agree on a successor. Their disagreement would permanently split Islam.

In 2015, approximately 10 percent of the world's nearly 1.8 billion Muslims were Shi'ite and 90 percent were Sunni.[3] Aside from the successorship question, the groups agree on most things. However, some differences in interpreting and applying the teachings exist. One significant difference is the two types of leadership, Imams and caliphates. Shi'ites see the Imams, who are of the Prophet's bloodline, as divinely inspired and thus infallible for guiding the Muslim community. This inspiration enables Imams to adapt Muhammad's teachings (including those now in the Koran) and those of

Some copies of the Koran are written in elegant Arabic script.

Imams from the early days of Islam to interpret modern situations, Shi'ites argue. The Sunni caliphs, on the other hand, are elected leaders. Their authority isn't religious, but political and military.

The Rightly Guided Caliphs

Several followers advised 'Ali to insist on his right to lead. They rejected Abu Bakr and anyone besides 'Ali. However, 'Ali chose not to stir discord. Some Sunnis believe he accepted Abu Bakr's leadership, while Shi'ite historians believe being pushed aside distressed him.

In any case, Abu Bakr died in just two years, but not before appointing 'Umar ibn al-Khattab to succeed him. A slave assassinated 'Umar in 644. Then a council elected 'Uthman ibn 'Affan as caliph. 'Uthman extended the reach of Islam during his reign. He is also thought to be responsible for gathering the most reliable recordings of Muhammad's revelations (preserved at that point in the memory of the Prophet's followers) and destroying alternative written accounts so that there would be but one Koran considered authoritative. However, this version still allows for many of the differing interpretations that continue to stir debate and conflict in Islam today.

Dissension arose among the Muslims under 'Uthman because some believed he favored his relatives, didn't deal fairly with those who served him, and loved wealth. When 'Uthman was assassinated in 656, many again urged 'Ali to take his place, which he did. 'Ali himself was then assassinated in 661. These four caliphs became known as the Rightly Guided caliphs because they had learned under Muhammad.

ASHURA AND THE MARTYRDOM OF HUSAYN

Men march the streets of Iran and other Shi'a strongholds ritually cutting or beating themselves with chains until blood flows during Ashura. It is a day of mourning the martyrdom of Muhammad's grandson, Husayn, child of 'Ali and Fatimah. Since Shi'ites believe in successorship through the Prophet's family, early Shi'ites felt Husayn should have headed the faith, and they promised to help him become caliph. But Muawiyah ruled as fifth caliph, and then appointed his son, Yazid ibn al-Muhallab, as his successor, thereby breaking the Sunni practice of electing caliphs. In 680, thousands of Yazid's soldiers attacked Husayn, who was traveling with men, women, and children, at Karbala. Husayn and his men fought bravely but were massacred. The soldiers captured the women and children. Husayn followers in nearby Kufah failed to join them in battle, so the self-punishing of Ashura also represents inherited guilt. Many contemporary Muslim leaders discourage the bloody reenactments, feeling that they make a spectacle of Shi'a Islam. Some argue that donating blood on Ashura would serve a higher purpose.

The years of the Rightly Guided caliphs started a great wave of expansion for Islam. The Muslims unified the entire Arabian Peninsula under Islam, as well as modern-day Syria, Iraq, Persia (in modern-day Iran), the Fertile Crescent, Egypt, Libya, and parts of Armenia. They aimed not necessarily to spread religion as much as to spread a better way of life. Muhammad had told them people should be Muslims because of true belief, not coerced conversion. The conquered peoples could follow their own religions and were guaranteed protection from enemies if they paid a tax. Muslim rule created a peace and prosperity the regions had seen little of. This peace and the example the Muslims set in following their own teachings attracted many converts. Among other principles, Islam promoted equality, regardless of kinship or skin color, as well as a higher position for women.

Breakaway Movements of the Umayyad Period

The vast area the Muslims had conquered became an empire. From 661 through 750, the Umayyad dynasty ruled it. During this dynasty, Islamic territory expanded into North Africa, what are now Spain and Portugal, parts of Europe, and the Indian subcontinent. The empire's capital moved to the busy capital city of Damascus in what is now Syria. As Arabic became the government's language, people were better able to exchange ideas, helping the already advanced capital city become greater still.

However, the period also brought about rebellion. Non-Muslims and even non-Arab Muslims paid heavier taxes than Arab Muslims. Non-Arab Muslims especially became increasingly frustrated, as they believed the extra taxes went against what the Koran said about equality. The Kharijites, a radical Islamic sect responsible for 'Ali's death, were intent on militantly applying the Koran's teachings. For them, the world was divided between believers and unbelievers. If someone sinned, they felt they should punish the person until he or she repented, or else kill the person. Though this early sect of Islam died out in the 700s, it became a model for future radical groups.

Another group that began as an unnamed trend during Muhammad's time gained its name in this period. The Sufis come from both the Shi'a and Sunni traditions. These mystical followers spend their time in prayer, contemplation, and voluntary poverty. Their approach became known as Sufism. The Arabic word *suf* means "wool." The name was based on the rough woolen clothing some wore. Concerned with purifying themselves in order to approach God, they saw themselves as focusing on

Qasr 'Amrah is a fortress built during the Umayyad dynasty in what is now Jordan.

Muhammad's core teachings. Sufis tend to be compassionate. Many are accepting of all religions, and they often work to spread peace in the world.

The Abbasid Dynasty

Abu Muslim, a freed slave, led a revolt that was backed by many Shi'ites, eventually bringing an end to the Umayyad era. Abu al-Abbas, a descendant of Muhammad's uncle, was named caliph, forming the Abbasid dynasty (750–1258). This new era became known as the golden age of the Islamic empire.

The capital moved to Baghdad, and religious focus turned inward. Artists, scholars, and merchants became highly respected. Christians and Jews held government positions alongside Muslims. They often joined forces when battles were necessary. Even intermarriage was accepted. The intermingling of these diverse cultures and nations led to a blending of ideas.

In what is now Iran, Persia's long tradition of beautiful art and poetry merged with Islamic ideals. Mathematics was made less laborious with the development of Arabic numerals, the decimal system, and the number zero in Persia, India, and Greece. These tools were popularized by Muslim

WHIRLING DERVISHES

In the 1200s, a poet named Jalal al-Din Rumi founded a division of Sufism called Mawlawiyah. Today these people are also known as the whirling dervishes. One of their practices includes praying while spinning to music. Rumi explained the mystical experience: "Dancing is when you rise above both worlds, tearing your heart to pieces and giving up your soul."[4] Their twirling dance imitates the revolutions of the natural world, such as the circling of planets and seasons. It leads to a trance state and feelings of submission and nearness to God.

writers. The world's first universities advanced science, medicine, philosophy, literature, architecture, and other arts. The oldest university still open is Qarawiyin, started by an Arab woman named Fatima al-Fihri in 859 CE. Scholars further advanced knowledge in the region by translating ancient and contemporary texts into Arabic.

Other areas also flourished. The paved streets of what is now the Spanish city of Córdoba boasted 70 libraries—the ruler's library alone contained 400,000 books—and hundreds of mosques and public baths.[5] By contrast, most of Europe struggled through what is now called the Middle Ages from the 400s through the 1400s. After the fall of the Roman Empire and economic devastation, most people worked under a system that kept

PERSPECTIVES

RABI'A AL-'ADAWIYYA

Sufis do not discriminate between men and women. Both are capable of a worship-filled life, and thus there are many female Sufi saints. Rabi'a al-'Adawiyya of the 700s in Iraq is noteworthy among the earliest saints. As no one wrote about her until centuries after her passing, separating legend from fact is difficult. But Sufis tell of many miraculous events involving Rabi'a. She is thought to have been orphaned as a child and sold into slavery. One night, her master saw her praying and observed a glow above her head lighting the whole house. The next day he set her free.

Rabi'a, a beautiful Sufi master, or teacher, refused all marriage proposals. Marriage, she believed, would distract her from worshipping the Beloved, as she called God. Explaining her decision, she wrote:

My peace, O my brothers, is in solitude,

And my Beloved is with me alway, [sic]

For His love I can find no substitute.[6]

Qarawiyin houses a mosque as well as a university.

them uneducated and poor. Only the upper class had access to the limited store of literature. Public baths, aside from natural waterways, were absent until this population came in contact with more advanced Islamic civilizations.

The Abbasid empire was not all glory and advancement, however. There were corrupt leaders who ruled with a heavy hand and frequently used the royal executioner, even while supporting development. There were also attacks from dissenting Muslim groups. Then, the golden age of Islam came to an end with the Crusades and the invasion of Mongolians under Genghis Khan.

The Crusades

Many of the wars plaguing Islam's early years were initiated by other groups, including Christians. The Crusades (1095–1453), a series of brutal campaigns, began with Pope Urban II, who desired to strengthen his authority, and Alexius I, a Byzantine emperor who had been badly beaten by the Abbasids in battle. Religion provided an excuse for wars largely motivated by politics, military ambition, and economics. As religious studies scholars John L. Esposito, Darrell J. Fasching, and Todd Lewis say, the West generally has subscribed to "three

ISLAMIC ARCHITECTURE

Muhammad encouraged his followers to follow his example and build when he toted bricks to build his mosque and helped build homes for other Muslims. It was not until Islam was well established in an area and the economy allowed for new construction that distinctive styles of architecture began to develop. Gradually, art, architecture, and belief came together in buildings using arches, domes, columns, minarets (narrow towers), and interior courtyards. Much of the beauty of Islamic architecture is seen in its complex geometric designs and calligraphy on the walls and ceilings. Islamic architecture has been much overlooked by Western architects and writers.

BELOVED PERSIAN POET HAFIZ

Born in approximately 1320, Sufi Shams al-Din Muhammad Hafiz, the pride of Persia, is commonly called Hafiz. The title *Hafiz* indicates he memorized the Koran. As a young man, his poetry achieved national recognition. Daniel Ladinsky translated many of Hafiz's poems in the book *I Heard God Laughing*. Among them is "Manic Screaming," a poem that attempts to simplify a spiritual problem, explaining that suffering is caused by our not wanting to buy what God has to sell. The manic screaming is a result of our insistent bargaining over cost.

myths" about the Crusades: that Muslims began the conflict, that Christians won, and that liberating Jerusalem from Muslim rule was the goal.[7] None of these, they say, are true.

Although Islam accepted Jesus as a prophet and allowed Christians in their midst to practice their religion, the Christian world did not accept Islam. Muhammad, after all, came long after Jesus, claiming an additional message from God. By the 1000s, more and more people followed Islam, and those who lived among Muslims but retained their religions often absorbed much of Arabic culture. It worried Christians in Europe, and so the prospect of a war to regain Jerusalem, a city holy to Christians, Muslims, and Jews alike, stirred Christians' interest.

At the outset, the Christians won Jerusalem, slaughtering Jews as they journeyed and, in the holy city, massacring women and children along with male Muslims and Jews. A Muslim leader, Saladin, recaptured Jerusalem in 1187. Control of Jerusalem continually changed over the several hundred years the Crusades staggered on.

One positive outcome of the bloody years of the Crusades is that Europeans became more aware of the advancements of Islamic civilization. The Crusaders returned home with knowledge that would speed up advancement in their own societies, a process already under way. Trade expanded as well. But territorial gains made by the Christians were eventually lost, and the Crusades poisoned Islamic-Christian relations far into the future.

The Ottoman Empire (1299–1922)

In the chaos of battles during the 1200s, a Muslim group known as the Ottomans began building a new empire spreading from Asia Minor into parts of Europe. Their vast civilization lasted many centuries. The empire focused on military conquest. Those areas that fell under their rule often enjoyed fairer government than before, with taxes that no longer overburdened the peasants. But succession issues dogged these rulers as they had from Islam's beginnings, creating frequent turmoil.

The cultures of the Ottoman Empire varied. However, in time, the rulers began restoring features from Islam's golden age and adding to them, especially in architecture, poetry, ceramics, and carpet making. It was during this period that the Muslim ruler of India built a tomb, the famous Taj Mahal, for his beloved wife. The magnificent Suleymaniye Mosque in Turkey was also built during the Ottomans' time.

This civilization lasted for centuries because of its strength. But it was an unwieldy empire, lacking modern transportation and communication methods, and it had enemies both Christian and Muslim.

Istanbul, in what is now Turkey, was the capital of the Ottoman Empire.

Moreover, its rulers' increasing wealth and corruption led to internal disputes. The Ottomans also failed to keep pace with advancing science, technology, and commerce in the West, adding to the problems that, together, led to the empire's collapse in the wake of World War I (1914–1918).

Reforming Islam

The competing interests and rulers, often straying far from Islamic principles, produced many reform movements. Among the most prominent was Saudi Arabia's Wahhabi movement of the mid-1700s. Its leader, Muhammad ibn 'Abd al-Wahhab, condemned everything straying from the Prophet's original teachings. This included war among tribes, Sufis' focus on the next world, and saint worship, which he felt was contrary to the belief in one God. Wahhab joined with a tribal chief who engineered a war to reunite Arabia and restore what he considered true Islam. They destroyed the tombs of Muhammad and other early believers, creating bitter feelings in other Muslim communities.

The Mahdiyya group in Sudan, now a nation in northern Africa, also gained many followers. Its Sufi leader, Muhammad Ahmad, claimed divine authority based on the Koran's promise that a Mahdi, a "divinely guided one," would begin an era of justice and renewed religion.[8] Despite the Sufi connection, this group saw holy war as appropriate and took control of Sudan in the late 1800s, establishing strict laws. Ahmad ruled until his death in 1885, and the government was soon overthrown.

CORE BELIEFS

Muhammad's message calls humanity back to teachings given by earlier prophets, from Adam to Abraham and Moses to Jesus. The most significant, perhaps, is the belief in one God, whose teachings have been revealed to humanity over time. Muslims, then, feel a connection with Christianity and Judaism. A passage in the Koran, sura (or chapter) 29 verse 46 (29:46), instructs Muslims, "dispute ye not with the People of the Book."[1] The People of the Book are Christians and Jews who also have part of God's revelation. But Muslims believe the original teachings of these faiths have been corrupted, distorted, or lost over time. Muslims believe the Koran corrects such issues and adds new teachings, completing previous revelations.

Muslims point to Bible verses as prophesying the coming of Muhammad. One verse, depending on the translation, speaks of an advocate or comforter who will come after Jesus. In the New Testament, the book of John, chapter 14 verse 26 (14:26), reads, "But

Muslims handle the Koran with respect. They do not set it on the floor or stack other books on top of it.

THE LAST PROPHET

In the mid-1800s, some Shi'ites did not believe Muhammad was the last prophet. They expected the return of the Twelfth Imam, also called the Mahdi. In 1844, a Persian descendant of Muhammad using the title Bab, meaning "gate" in Arabic, claimed prophethood. He stated his mission as preparing the way for another messenger from God, the one promised by the world's religions to unite humanity and guide them to create the kingdom of God on Earth, an era of peace and justice.

One of the Bab's followers took the title Baha'u'llah, or "Glory of God." This man announced in 1863 that he was that promised one. From a Muslim family, he was a descendant of Abraham. Baha'u'llah explained Muhammad's title, "Seal of the Prophet," differently: the age of prophecy had ended; his and the Bab's revelations began a new cycle, the age of fulfillment. As did Muhammad, Baha'u'llah confirmed past revelations but added others, incorporating aspects of Hinduism and Buddhism. He also brought new teachings addressing modern life. The religion is independent from Islam, just as Islam is from Christianity. Today, the Baha'i faith has spread around the globe; its followers, called Baha'is, are of every walk of life and all races. Believers strive to live their lives according to Baha'u'llah's teachings while upholding his principle of retaining and celebrating cultural differences. Their leadership is composed of elected, temporary positions rather than a clergy since Baha'u'llah explained that individuals can read and understand the teachings for themselves. As a result, Baha'is feel individually responsible to take up the tasks that might ordinarily be assumed by clergy—visiting the sick, sharing the faith, and studying its teachings.

the Advocate, the Holy Spirit, whom the Father will send in my name, will teach you all things and will remind you of everything I have said to you."[2] Indeed, the Koran does recount many biblical stories.

While Muhammad is not viewed as divine, the Koran says he was the "Messenger of Allah, and the Seal of the Prophets."[3] The statement that Muhammad is the seal of the prophets indicates he is the final prophet, bringing the last word from God. The Twelvers, a group within the Shi'a, believe 12 hereditary Imams followed Muhammad until 874. At that time, the twelfth Imam was hidden, to return some distant day. Sometimes called the promised Mahdi, he will establish an era of justice and peace and prepare people for Judgment Day. This is the doctrine followed by the government of Iran.

Angels, Jinns, Satan, and the Afterlife

Islam, Christianity, and Judaism all share angels, including the angel Gabriel, who revealed the Koran to Muhammad. Angels worship God and can appear in human form to do his bidding. They can interact with God's prophets and with ordinary people. The Koran also teaches the existence of Satan, who was either once an angel who disobeyed God or one of the jinns. The jinns are thinking beings ranked between angels and people and are capable of good and evil. They are aware of people and may disrupt or help them, though people cannot see them. The fact that jinns are mentioned in the Koran gives them much credibility among Muslims, as the Koran is the word of God. In sura 55:33, for example, Muhammad addresses the jinns directly: "O ye assembly of Jinns And men! If it be Ye can pass beyond The zones of the heavens And the earth, pass ye!"[4]

Muslims also believe in an afterlife. According to the Koran, people are resurrected from the grave on Judgment Day, when the world ends and God evaluates them. The two great sins are to worship anything other than, or along with, God, as well as ingratitude toward or disbelief in God. People might commit these sins and later repent and believe, and God would forgive them. Essentially, people's actions and thoughts determine their position in the afterlife. Believers will enjoy the heaven

of God's nearness. Unbelievers will be condemned to the hell of distance from him. Much has been made of the Islamic promises of heaven filled with beautiful women, delicious food, and comfort, but most consider this symbolic of things people have not experienced yet, rather than being a literal description. As for those believers assigned to hell, God in his mercy will lift them to heaven in time. Unbelievers will remain in hell. These promises of reward or punishment, along with Muhammad's other teachings, give Muslims strong signals about how to live. Those who live good and holy lives can be assured of reward.

Muslims throughout Islam's history have imagined what jinns might look like, as in this illustration from the 1300s.

God can send people to heaven or hell because people are responsible for themselves. God is omniscient, so he knows how his creatures will behave. God is also loving, involved in people's lives, and has a plan for humanity. Imam Kamil Mufti, a notable American Muslim scholar, believes that "God's foreknowledge is infallible." Yet within this, there is freedom. The Imam continues, "Man must have within his power the ability to break or keep the law. God would not hold us responsible for something unless we were capable of doing it."[5]

WHICH SON?

Jews, Christians, and Muslims all teach that God commanded Abraham to sacrifice his only son. But they disagree about who that son was. The Old Testament and Hebrew Bible identify that son as Abraham's second son, Isaac. According to the New Testament, his family line leads to Jesus. However, the Koran identifies him as Ishmael, whose line leads to Muhammad. Imam Kamil Mufti argues that Ishmael was Abraham's firstborn son, the only one who could, temporarily, be called the only son, suggesting that the biblical story was altered. Whichever son it was, both texts agree that Abraham readied himself to follow God's command, and God stopped him before he accomplished it, sparing the son's life.

THE PRACTICE OF ISLAM

The religious laws of Islam are known as Sharia. The term *Sharia*, Arabic for "path to water," is based on the Koran and stories of Muhammad's example. It guides believers in their actions before God and among each other. It addresses methods of worship and restricts alcohol, sexual activity outside of marriage, certain meats, and gambling, along with other requirements to benefit individuals and communities. For example, Sharia protects property rights for men and women. Along with securing rights, Sharia encourages qualities including justice, kindness, and charity.

Sharia law has been misunderstood in the West. The media often overlooks Western law's harshest punishments, while those of Sharia receive much attention. Sharia brought civility and morality to a lawless people who once held loyalty only to tribe and kin. Through it, the practice of killing unwanted children, frequent

Sharia is interpreted differently around the world. In Indonesia, a man may be whipped for unlawfully touching a woman he isn't married to. Other Muslims may find this extreme.

wars, drunkenness, and other social ills were greatly reduced as people tried to follow Muhammad's teachings. According to Sana Tayyen, a visiting scholar and professor at the University of Southern California and the University of Redlands, many Muslims do not believe the harshest punishments in Sharia should be used today. The examples many people see on the news are extreme and do not represent how most Muslims practice Sharia. Sharia is not applicable to non-Muslims. Some Westerners think that Sharia discriminates against women, but as Tayyen explains, it instead sees the genders as complementary. She says, "Muslim women do have their own struggles among their Muslim brethren and have to fight for their rights, this is no different than Western women fighting for their rights of equal pay and freedom from sexual harassment. Even within Sharia, women are arguing that certain things need to change and they are becoming Islamic law jurists and judges."[1]

HOW SHARIA LAW IS DETERMINED

Islamic law comes from four sources, the first being the Koran. The Koran is made up of 114 suras of approximately 6,000 verses from the revelations Muhammad received across a period of 22 years.[2] Examples from Muhammad also influence Sharia. These examples are called the Sunna. The Sunna comes from hadiths, which include early biographies, histories, and his sayings passed on orally from witnesses. When neither the Koran nor the Sunna offers clear counsel, religious scholars decide based on justice, custom, and the community's needs. If the answer is still not easily decided, a group of scholars come to an agreement on important decisions.

The Five Pillars of Islam

The word *Islam* is Arabic for "submission." The idea is that God's followers should submit to their maker to please and draw closer to him. The main means of doing so is through the Five Pillars of Islam—practices that Muslims all over the world take to heart.

The first pillar is the Shahada, meaning to proclaim belief. Muslims often say, "There is no God but Allah, and Muhammad is his messenger."[3] Muslims feel an obligation to let others know about their religion so non-Muslims can make an informed choice.

Salah, or praying five times a day, is the second pillar. In cities with large Muslim populations, a cry of "God is Most Great" from mosque minarets summons people to prayer at dawn, noon, midafternoon, sunset, and evening.[4] Muslims may

PRAYER RUGS OR MATS

When praying, many Muslims use prayer rugs. From the time Muhammad laid out a palm frond and reed mat on which to kneel and lay his head during prayer, prayer rugs, mats, or cloths have been a standard possession for believers. Muslims prepare for prayer by ritually washing themselves. The prayer rugs also provide a clean surface for prostrations. Early on, prayer rugs depicted a door to heaven with an arch pointing to Mecca. Columns and trees of life were other popular design elements. A person could determine the maker's tribe or city by early designs. Today, designs are more varied and mass-produced.

An Imam leads prayers in front of worshippers while facing Mecca.

stop wherever they are, wash their faces and hands, turn in the direction of Mecca, and offer prayers. Or they may join in prayers led by an Imam at a mosque or elsewhere. There they stand shoulder to shoulder with other believers, heedless of status, separated only by gender. Each worshipper has a small prayer rug for praying. Muslims begin prayer by standing on the rug facing Mecca. Then they follow a series of positions. They bow and straighten up again. They prostrate with their foreheads, noses, palms, knees, and toes touching the rug. They kneel on the rug. These positions intensify feelings of devotion.

Just as Muslims owe submission to God, so too are they responsible for their community. Unless unable, they must give some of their earnings to the needy. This third pillar, called Zakat, helps reduce poverty, encourage concern for others, and prevent greed.

The Ramadan fast, or Sawm, is the fourth pillar. The fast is observed only by healthy individuals—children and those who

are sick or weak, pregnant, nursing, or menstruating are all excused from fasting. The fast is a spiritual discipline intended to bring believers closer to God.

The fifth and final pillar is a one-time obligation. This is hajj, a pilgrimage to the Kaaba. There is no fault against the poor or others who cannot comply. Tradition holds that Abraham and his son Ishmael created the Kaaba, now housed in Mecca's Great Mosque. Hajj occurs two months and ten days after Ramadan. Wrapped in white cloth that erases signs of status, as many as three million pilgrims from around the world approach the city annually with calls of "I am here, O Lord, I am here!" They circle the Kaaba seven times and perform other rites of pilgrimage.[5]

Jihad

Some Muslims have added a sixth pillar, called *jihad,* which is Arabic for "striving" or "struggle." The popular Western press interprets it as holy war, and contemporary extremist groups feed this idea. But most Muslims view it differently. They

PERSPECTIVES

AN AMERICAN MUSLIM'S PILGRIMAGE

After years of directing prayers toward Mecca, Rubaina Azhar of the *Los Angeles Times* was eager to visit the Kaaba. When she and her family joined the crowds circling the Kaaba, Azhar was glad when she finally touched the sacred building. But the heart of the pilgrimage, she says, is a day of prayer in Arafat, a desert plain. Azhar had never attempted a whole day of prayer. She remarked, "It was humbling to see so many worshippers break down in tears as they sought God's guidance and mercy." For herself, this time was "emotionally draining." She explains, "There was no going-through-the-motions at Arafat. I meant my prayers. I felt them."[7]

Because of prejudice against Islam and misunderstanding she's felt in the United States, she had thought it might be easier to be Muslim in a Muslim-majority country. Now a hajji, one who has made the pilgrimage, she concludes, "America is my home. I'm not interested in moving to Saudi Arabia or any other Muslim country. But I'm grateful to have felt, because of the godsend journey of hajj, a part of global Islam."[8]

define it as overcoming one's own ego to live a peaceful, harmonious life in keeping with Islamic teachings. They try to avoid selfishness, jealousy, and greed. This is what the Prophet Muhammad called the Greater Jihad. It takes steady effort and deep understanding of the teachings.

The Lesser Jihad is defense of the community, life, faith, and honor. This can involve armed fighting. Coming from the society in which Islam formed, Muhammad needed to discuss war. Sura 22:39 explains, "To those against whom War is made, permission is given (to fight), because They are wronged."[6] In other words, if the community is attacked, it has the right to defend itself. "But if they [the aggressors] cease, Allah is Oft-Forgiving," explains sura 2:192. Sura 2:193 adds, "Let there

ACTIVIST FARID ESACK

The South Africa of Farid Esack's youth was wrapped in apartheid, a system of racial oppression that kept people of color poor and powerless. Though Muslims were scarcely more than 1 percent of the population, in 1984, Esack established the Call of Islam to fight apartheid, gender inequality, and environmental destruction. He also encouraged diverse groups to work together. At times, Esack lived as a fugitive to escape imprisonment and attack by police and their dogs. Still, he continued spreading hope for a just society. Esack takes courage from sura 47:7 of the Koran: "If you assist Allah, then He will assist you."[11] He explains, "For me, this meant that I had to participate in a struggle for freedom and justice and, if I wanted God's help in this, then I had to assist him."[12]

On September 11, 2001, terrorists who identified as Muslims attacked the Pentagon in Washington, DC, and New York's World Trade Center. In response to the attacks, the US media often called on Esack to shed light on Islamic thinking. He observes that many Muslims look to Mecca, where Muslims were persecuted, and to Medina, where they ruled, for guidelines on how to live in different situations. The Abyssinian model, he notes, offers an attractive third alternative of living cooperatively with other religions. It draws inspiration from the Christian Abyssinian king who protected Muslims and allowed them to live peacefully alongside Christians.

be no hostility Except to those Who practice oppression."[9] A hadith (a report of Muhammad's words and deeds) notes, "the preferred jihad is a truth spoken in presence of a tyrant."[10]

EAST MEETS WEST

Muslims have a long history in the United States. The first enslaved African Muslims arrived in the 1500s. Esposito, Fasching, and Lewis estimate that 20 percent of slaves brought into the country from the 1500s through the 1800s were Muslim.[1] Not all Muslims were from Africa, however. In time, other free Arab Muslims came, followed by Muslims from elsewhere in the Middle East and from South Asia. They sought work, schooling, or freedom from conflict at home. Among the first American converts to Islam was Alexander Russell Webb, who encountered the religion in the Philippines. On his return to New York, he founded the American Islamic Mission in 1893. Muslims have lived in parts of Europe nearly from the religion's beginnings.

In the early 1900s, many African Americans discussed how Christianity had been twisted to justify slavery in the United States.

During the 1960s and 1970s, Islam influenced many high-profile people, including famed boxer Muhammad Ali, *light suit*.

MALCOLM X AND THE NATION OF ISLAM

One of the best-known members of the Nation of Islam was Malcolm Little. After joining the movement, he replaced his surname, handed down from slave owners, with X in 1952. This was a common practice for members of the Nation of Islam. Born in poverty and headed for a life of crime, Malcolm transformed his life through Islam. He was a fiery speaker who rejected white rule and preached a militant response to racism, countering Martin Luther King Jr.'s peaceful protests. However, Malcolm's pilgrimage to Mecca showed him Muslims of all races mingling in harmony, and he embraced unity. He broke from the Nation of Islam and converted to Sunni Islam. In 1965, three members of the Nation of Islam assassinated Malcolm.

They turned to statements from the Koran that support equality, such as sura 30:22: "And among His wonders is the creation of the heavens and the earth, and the diversity of your tongues and colors."[2] Sura 6:98 states that God created all people from one person. If any doubt remained, Muhammad's "Farewell Sermon" added: "All mankind is from Adam and Eve . . . a white has no superiority over black nor a black has any superiority over white except by piety . . . and good action."[3]

Many African Americans became interested in Islam. They realized that, had they been left in their ancestral lands, they might have been raised Muslim. Eventually, black nationalism, a movement to create an independent black nation, combined with borrowed elements of Islam to become a group called the Nation of Islam in the 1930s. The Nation of Islam drew growing numbers of young African Americans as the civil rights movement gathered momentum in the 1950s and 1960s. They were called Black Muslims. In addition to advocating for self-rule, they armed themselves in defense of African American communities, who were often the target of uncalled-for police violence. By the 1980s, following a change in leadership, the group members brought themselves more in line with Sunni Islam. They redefined themselves as the American Muslim Mission, accepting racial and gender equality and more closely following Islamic practices, such as observing the Five Pillars.

The Muslim Brotherhood

Islam also interacted with Western ideas in the Middle East. Tension between the Eastern and Western parts of the world has its roots in European imperialism throughout much of the Islamic world. With colonization came missionaries trying to convert people to Christianity. Individuals and countries responded differently to encroaching westernization. Some adapted, eventually leading to such changes as advocating separating religion from government, sending youth to study in the West, and Western-style dress. However, others resented and fought against the loss of Muslim rule and dismissal of their religion, along with the attitude of superiority both colonizers and missionaries often brought.

In Egypt, Hassan al-Banna, a young teacher, became part of the Islamic Revivalism of the 1920s and 1930s when he created the Muslim Brotherhood in 1928. Egypt had been under British rule since the late 1800s. Al-Banna hoped to restore the strength and self-government of Islam. The Brotherhood began by providing programs centered on religion and education. Soon it formed a militia called the Special Apparatus. The Brotherhood grew, and its Special Apparatus made itself known through terrorism.

Al-Banna was assassinated in 1949. The new leader assured the government that the militia had been disbanded. In reality, the Special Apparatus had simply transformed itself. Other terrorist groups formed under Islam's banner with Brotherhood support. One group bombed New York's World Trade Center in 1993, protesting US support of Israel in a conflict with Palestine. Six died and more than 1,000 were injured.[4] The Brotherhood's philosophy spread as members moved from nation to nation. Others who held to Islamist thought—that government and society at large should follow the Koran and hadiths—joined its ranks.

A new International Apparatus helped create the impression that by jihad, Muhammad meant attacking those with differing opinions. The group recruited members in the West, planning to disrupt Western armies, schools, and governments. It became key in launching political Islam, a movement often called Islamic fundamentalism, in the late 1960s.

Political Islam

Political Islam, beginning in the 1960s, grew out of the disappointment many Muslims felt as their countries began to adopt Western ideals. They had hoped association with the West would translate into a higher standard of living. However, the poverty, lack of education, and unemployment plaguing

The 1993 World Trade Center bombing left a crater several stories deep.

Muslim-majority countries were not so easily solved. Many Muslims yearned for Islam's glory as an empire during the Abbasid dynasty. They hoped that as their nations limited foreign influence, Islam's influence in the world would be restored.

When their hopes were not realized, some responded by rekindling their religious commitment. Others turned to political Islam. Political Islam was quite varied. Some people took a moderate position, while others adopted extremism, alarming both moderate Muslims and Western non-Muslims. The activists agreed on several points, however. First, they believed that Islam should guide both religious and civic life. Laws and modern development should agree with the Koran and the Prophet's example. They also blamed Muslim-majority countries' decline on the Western separation of religion and government.

The Iranian Revolution (1978–1979) vividly demonstrated the shift away from friendship with the West toward opposition. Discontent brewed in Iran for many reasons. Many objected to government corruption, repression, and a perceived anti-Islamic bias. They also faced social problems including unemployment and inflation. The popular exiled religious leader Ayatollah Khomeini urged citizen groups to clash with the police. Eventually, the fighting forced the Shah—a form of king—and his family to seek refuge in the West. Khomeini soon led Iran's new government, an Islamic republic. The result was a very narrow view of Islamic law enforced by police and even more repression.

By the late 1980s and into the 1990s, most Muslim-majority countries limited or completely rejected Western cultural influence and domination and refocused on Islam. While they did not object to modernization, they felt it should be guided by Islamic values. News reports of hijacked airplanes, bombed embassies, and kidnappings stirred alarm over radical Islamic fundamentalism in the West and among moderate Muslim leaders. Moderate Muslims were also troubled by radical groups' demands for leadership in government. Many radicals gained government positions.

Al-Qaeda and 9/11

Nothing, however, captured global concern like the attacks on New York's World Trade Center and the Pentagon in Washington, DC, on September 11, 2001 (9/11). Saudi Arabian terrorist leader Osama bin Laden and his group, al-Qaeda, planned the attack. Al-Qaeda, formed in the 1980s, grew out of its founders' concerns about a cultural takeover in Islamic lands by the West, as well as their desire to return to the roots of Islam. While Saudi Arabia was an Islamist nation, bin Laden and others objected to its military agreements and other ties with the United States. As did

Iranians held marches to protest the government during the Iranian Revolution.

al-Banna's Muslim Brotherhood, al-Qaeda saw jihad as a command to fight nonbelievers.

On 9/11, al-Qaeda terrorists took control of four US airliners. Two struck and destroyed the 110-story Twin Towers of the World Trade Center, a complex of offices in New York City. A third plane destroyed part of the Pentagon, the country's military headquarters. Investigators believe the fourth was headed for the US Capitol building, but crew and passengers overcame the hijackers, crashing the plane. While all on board died, they saved many lives at the intended target. In all, the attacks claimed 2,996 lives, including 19 terrorists.

Although this wasn't the first foreign attack on US soil, 9/11 caused the greatest loss of civilians in US history and rocked the nation's sense of security. President George W. Bush responded by beginning what he called the War on Terror, which later included the Iraq War (2003–2011). The military invaded Afghanistan, al-Qaeda's headquarters. Forces also unseated the Taliban, the extremist group that had gained leadership in the country and welcomed bin Laden's group. US troops found and killed bin Laden in 2011.

America Reacts to 9/11

Shocked to have been attacked so boldly on the US mainland, many Americans responded with fear and anger. The term *Islamophobia* was used to name the distrust of all things Islamic, as well as violence against Muslims. Women wearing hijabs were sometimes attacked simply because of their visibility as Muslims. Media coverage of Islam was generally negative, and the media rarely invited Muslims as experts when their religion was discussed.

Yet despite the Islamist terrorists and hate-mongering, one study revealed the Muslim population in the United States more than doubled between 2000 and 2010. In 2000, 1 million Muslims called the US home, growing to 2.6 million ten years later.[5] While immigration caused much of that increase, the attention to Islam led many Americans to study the religion. When they found that Muhammad preached not hate and violence but unity between races, gender equality, and peacefulness, some converted.

US soldiers hadn't planned on helping one of the most brutal terrorist groups form when they imprisoned violent jihadists in Iraq. But as one young radical explained, imprisonment gave them a safe space to consult with other radicals. There, al-Qaeda leader Abu Musab al-Zarqawi became leader of the Islamic State in Iraq and Syria (ISIS). After his release, the group attacked a Shi'ite Islamic shrine in Iraq in 2006, sparking violence between Shi'ites and Sunnis. When the United States killed al-Zarqawi in an air strike that same year, other leaders quickly stepped in. The group's aim is to establish its own rule. ISIS fighters attack cities to gain control and spread their power. They continue to use violence, including public executions and physical harm, to keep conquered areas under ISIS control.

THE ARAB SPRING

In 2011, a wave of uprisings in African and Middle Eastern nations seemed to promise a new era of freedom and democracy. Called the Arab Spring, it began when a young Tunisian street vendor, harassed by police, set himself on fire in protest. Others, mostly youth, picked up the martyr's cause. News of the protests quickly spread through internet posts. The Tunisian ruler fled, which set off successful protests toppling leaders in Egypt, Libya, and Yemen. However, the older, well-organized radical Islamist groups succeeded in getting their candidates into office, cooling the optimism of that time.

TRUMP'S TRAVEL BAN

Soon after Donald Trump became president in January 2017, he announced a ban on people from seven Muslim-majority countries from entering the United States: Iran, Iraq, Libya, Somalia, Sudan, Syria, and Yemen. Much protest greeted the announcement. Many felt the ban, which made an exception for Syrian Christians, was a religious ban and therefore against American values. They also pointed out that no terror-related deaths in the United States had been caused by extremists from the named countries. Forced to rethink his order, Trump came up with a revised list de-emphasizing the Muslim connection in September 2017: Chad, Iran, Libya, North Korea, Somalia, Syria, Venezuela, and Yemen. Though the ban was announced as being a protective measure against dangerous people, it had more widespread effects. Other people affected by this order included tourists, patients needing specialized medical care, and individuals with relatives in the United States. The numbers of refugees fleeing war and other crises in their homelands were cut to less than half of what had been allowed under the previous president, Barack Obama. Arguments from both sides of the issue made their way to the Supreme Court into 2018, hoping to sway the judges' final decision on the ban's legality.

Muslim Response to Terrorism

According to a 2017 Pew Research Center study, 82 percent of Muslim Americans are concerned about the spread of so-called Islamist terrorism. Muslims, particularly women and those ages 55 and up, express even greater concern about global terrorism.[6] Some Muslim-majority nations also show widespread disapproval. For example, 94 percent of Jordanians and nearly all Lebanese people condemn ISIS.[7]

As seen in the 2006 ISIS shrine attack, terrorists target not only the West but also Muslims. The University of Maryland's Global Terrorism Database reveals that approximately half of all terrorist attacks from 2004 to 2013 targeted Afghanistan, Iraq, and Pakistan, all countries where most people are Muslim. These attacks resulted in 60 percent of all terror-related deaths, indicating that the majority of terrorists' victims are fellow Muslims.[8] As the struggle continues between fundamentalist and moderate Muslims, only time will tell which side will gain more prominence in the future.

DEBATES AND MISCONCEPTIONS

People in the West frequently hear about Islam in the context of terrorists and terrorism. Non-Muslim Westerners often do not know much about Islam or Muslims. People sometimes fear and distrust those who are different. Difference represents the unknown, and contact with the unknown can be unsettling. What people don't know and don't understand becomes "other," "not us," and therefore distant.

When people think through the unfamiliar culture's viewpoint, they often realize their first impressions were wrong. An example is the battles Muhammad and his early followers fought. Once, Western historians described Islam as being spread by the sword. Later, researchers realized the wars were defensive, that Muslims were caught in a society that forced them to fight. If Muslims in later times began battles, they were not observing their own teachings. But as

Western media tends to focus on extreme members of Islam, such as those belonging to ISIS, rather than the Muslims who fight the Islamic State, *pictured*.

the Muslim population in the West has grown, a fear of the unknown as well as clashing ways of life have led to challenges and misunderstandings.

Media's Role

While the media spreads information and understanding, it also plays a large role in spreading misinformation and misunderstanding. As Belinda F. Espiritu, who researches religion and communications, says, "It is the nature of media to report on the novel, the sensational, the bizarre, the dramatic, the extraordinary . . . occurrences of life. Hence . . . it does not report about peace-loving Muslims" but about actions of radicals who claim Islam. As a result, Islam is often portrayed as being at odds with Western civilization and paired with words such as "violent, fanatical . . . and terrorists."[1] An analysis of 345 separate studies on the issue found that most portrayals of Islam in the media focused on "'migration,' 'terrorism,' and 'war.'"[2]

DISNEY MOVIE STEREOTYPES

Coming from the time-honored *Arabian Nights* tales, Disney's *Aladdin* (1992) might seem to be a tribute to Arabic culture. But in reality, it set many Arab Americans and others sensitive to their portrayal on edge. An Arab American group that met with Disney officials succeeded in getting them to remove two objectionable lines from its opening song. However, the line "It's barbaric, but hey, it's home" still delivers a negative message to young viewers.[5] The movie features stereotypical brutal Arabs who attempt to cut off women's hands, and Aladdin himself is a thief.

The frightening villains look subhuman. Drake University's Professor Joanne Brown says they have "dark-hooded eyes and large hooked noses. Perhaps I am sensitive to this business of noses because I am Jewish."[6] Brown is alluding to German dictator Adolf Hitler's stereotyping of Jews to dehumanize them in the 1930s and early 1940s. To realize the damage such stereotypes do, Anthony Lane of the *New Yorker* suggests that those who stereotype Arabs could imagine substituting another racial group toward whom they are more sensitive. Despite protests against *Aladdin,* scholar Jack G. Shaheen notes that Disney went on to stereotype Arabs in *The Return of Jafar, Kazaam,* and other movies.

Movies are no exception. Professor Jack G. Shaheen, an international authority on the portrayal of Arabs in media, looked at more than 900 Hollywood films from across 100 years and found they dehumanized Muslim Arabs and portrayed them as lesser people.[4] Films tend to overlook Islam's diversity, portraying Muslims as always Arab. They are also, almost without exception, shown negatively. For example, *Tarzan of the Apes* (1918) shows Arabs abusing slaves. This was followed by *The Sheik* (1921), in which the lustful hero abducts any woman he wishes. Over time, notes Professor Rubina Ramji, portrayals of Muslim men shifted from backward, brutal, womanizing tyrants to "hijackers,

In *The Sheik*, an Arabian sheik kidnaps an Englishwoman he has fallen in love with.

kidnappers, and terrorists."[7] Muslim women transformed from belly dancers and harem girls to ghostly veil-draped figures.

Muhammad's Marriages

The role and rights of women also cause much confusion, beginning with the Prophet's own household. In Western countries that generally assume monogamy (one wife and one husband), understanding the polygyny (one man with multiple wives) of another time and place is difficult.

From all accounts, Muhammad and Khadijah's marriage was a loving partnership. A wealthy widow and businesswoman, Khadijah was unusual. She was 15 years older than Muhammad, and marrying him was her choice. Indeed, she suggested it. Muhammad turned to Khadijah after first encountering the angel Gabriel, and she continued to be a supportive friend and spouse. Throughout the 28 years of their marriage, she was Muhammad's only wife. However, after her death, Muhammad married additional women.

In the Prophet's time and culture, women were considered little better than animals. Some men debated whether they even had souls. A woman without money or a husband lived a hard life, and many were forced into prostitution to survive. Every woman needed a protector to establish her honor and provide for her. But an unmarried woman in a man's household would dishonor both. He must marry her. As in early biblical times, polygyny was standard practice.

After Khadijah's death, when Muhammad was approximately 50 years old, he married other women. Most were divorcees and widows of his followers who had died in battle. Some marriages helped build ties between diverse groups. In one case, Muslims had taken two hundred families as slaves after a battle. Muhammad freed the daughter of the defeated chief and married her. His example caused his followers to free the remaining slaves. The grateful tribe then embraced Islam. While Muhammad treated his wives with kindness and respect and enjoyed their companionship, he seemed to only truly love Aisha, the daughter of Abu Bakr. Despite multiple marriages, Muhammad fathered only one child after Khadijah died.

Marriages

Many argue that Muhammad prescribes monogamy, saying prophethood entitled him to additional marriages. He had 12 wives after Khadijah.[8] At a time when wealthy men could—and did—have hundreds of wives, the Koran limited wives to four with this advice in sura 4:3: "Marry women of your choice, Two, or three, or four; But if ye fear that ye shall not Be able to deal justly (with them), Then only one."[9] Many believe this indicates that, while it is best to have just one spouse, the Koran allows for situations such as Muhammad's when a man feels responsible for protecting other women. The Koran addresses the impossibility of equal treatment later in the sura: "Ye are never able To be fair and just as between women, Even if it is Your ardent desire."[10] Yet a hadith stresses the responsibility of men with

For Muslims, wedding clothes and ceremonies vary depending on the region. Brides in Turkey may wear red veils.

multiple spouses: "If a man has two wives and is inclined toward [favoring] one of them, then on the Day of Judgment he will be punished for his injustice."[11]

It is hard to say how many Muslim marriages actually do include multiple wives because polygamy is illegal in most countries. Men may add wives without documentation. In a 2013 survey of 37 nations, the Pew Research Center found most Muslims in sub-Saharan Africa accept the practice, but Muslims elsewhere express widespread disapproval. The Muslim author of the book *Islam Today*, Akbar S. Ahmed, echoes these reports, saying, "The vast majority of [Muslim] men are monogamous."[12]

The Koran does not speak directly about how a marriage should come about. Cultural traditions have filled in the gap, with some families arranging marriages for their children. Arranged marriages often face resistance in the West, where people believe it is not necessary to follow advice from family or friends in choosing a spouse. In an ideal arranged marriage, the parents look for someone who will be a good match for and take care of their son or daughter. Oftentimes, families accept that not every match will work out, in which case divorce is acceptable. But some families force their children into marriage even though Islamic law forbids this. A woman who does not follow her family's selection might face death for bringing the family dishonor. The controversies of arranged marriage rose to global attention in 2006 when Banaz Mahmod, a 20-year-old Iraqi Muslim living in the United Kingdom, was murdered by men her family had hired to kill her. She had left her abusive arranged marriage. Then she found a boyfriend. Mahmod had dishonored the family by divorcing and accepting a boyfriend without her family's approval. Mahmod's family members believed that only killing her would restore their honor. They considered her murder an honor killing.

"Honour killings are a direct outcome of forced marriage and have nothing to do with Islam," writes Ziauddin Sardar, chair of the Muslim Institute and editor of the publication *Critical Muslim*.[13] But a society's cultural practices and thinking tend to creep into believers' thinking and mingle with religion.

Over time, the lines between various traditions and Islam's teachings blur, and some Muslims believe practices such as forced marriages or honor killings are part of Islam, while others do not. Tragically, in Mahmod's case and similar ones, ancient practices clouded Islamic teachings.

In fact, Muhammad disapproved of both honor killings and forced marriages. Muhammad advocated for a woman's right to consent to or reject a marriage. Arranged marriage is different from a forced marriage, though. Aliyah Furqan experienced both the typical American love-based marriage and an arranged marriage. An American citizen, she fell in love

Mahmod's sister, Bekhal, testified against their father in court. He was convicted of murder.

A VERSE MISUNDERSTOOD

Sura 4:34 states that when a husband suspects his wife has been disloyal or acted badly, he is allowed, as a last resort, to "beat [her] (lightly)."[15] *Lightly* was not in the original Arabic, but added later, notes scholar Laleh Bakhtiar. Bakhtiar studied the Arabic term translated as *beat* and points out that it has multiple meanings, including "to avoid or shun . . . to be in a state between hope and fear; and to go away." The Prophet "never beat anyone," she argues.[16] Instead, she says, the Koran is instructing men to step back, cool off, and discuss the issue later. The Koran often advises husbands and wives to consult on differences.

with another student in her college's Muslim Student Association. It felt like the Hollywood-style romance she'd dreamed of. Though her parents weren't enthusiastic, they consented, and the couple married. Roughly a year later, the two realized that their feelings were fading and divorced.

Her parents chose her second husband, and she agreed. Unlike her first husband, he was committed to the relationship and showed her in many kind acts. Unlike her first husband, he was someone Furqan could count on. "Today I am a happily married woman," she reports. "Our life is not the stuff of which Hollywood chick flicks are made; rather, it is a series of small, insignificant, mundane events that weave together the fabric of our lives, making our bond stronger than I could ever have imagined."[14]

A parent's or guardian's consent to a marriage is usually required, especially for young women. In practice, however, some families do pressure young women to consent to a marriage. The family may have goals in mind other than the couple's compatibility, and the woman may be reluctant or even afraid to object.

Covering

Another point of controversy is women's clothing. Women are often the most public representatives of Islam because of veiling, or covering. Covering is part of the tradition of purdah, or seclusion, which stems from practices in pre-Islamic Persia, Mesopotamia, and the Mediterranean. Covering in public protected women from the gaze of unrelated men, as did separating men and women in cities. As with many religions, Islam encourages modesty for men as well as women. However, purdah was often interpreted as an appropriate response to the Prophet's teachings and, in many cases, was written into law.

Today, the degree of covering, as well as practices such as a woman needing a male relative to escort her in public, vary widely from place to place, by law, and by personal preference. The most common form of covering is a simple hijab, or head scarf. Some women choose more coverings for protection from unwanted attention. Others object to the restricted movement and feeling of invisibility but may be compelled by custom or law to wear them. A chador, for example, is a cloak, usually black, that is common in Iran. A woman uses a chador to cover all but her hands—which she

COVERINGS

hijab

chador

niqab

burqa

needs to close the cloak—and her face. A niqab, a full-body covering that shows only the eyes, is common in Saudi Arabia, while the blue burqa, a single piece of cloth worn in Afghanistan, includes a mesh screen blocking viewers from seeing a woman's eyes—and also hindering the woman's vision. Like the chador, women often need to hold the blue burqa closed with their hands. Some women in Afghanistan wear a three-piece black burqa. It allows more freedom of the hands and more areas for fresh air to enter under the cloth, making it easier to breathe. Many girls start out wearing the black burqa, but when they marry, their husbands' families might require them to wear the blue one. Some women respect these family traditions and agree. Others are more reluctant to lose the freedoms they had in the black burqa.

The debate often centers on how much a Muslim woman's clothing must cover. In the Koran, sura 24:31 says, "They should not display their beauty and ornaments except What (must ordinarily) appear Thereof."[17] They are to dress modestly by covering their chests except when with near relatives, other women, or small children. Defining the terms *beauty* and *ornaments* is key to the debate over covering. The various head coverings are cultural interpretations of the verse.

Many Muslims who use coverings believe the coverings help men treat women well and not objectify them sexually. Aliya Naim, a 20-year-old University of Georgia student, wore the hijab and loose-fitting clothing. "You often see in many societies women being objectified because of how they look or being disrespected," she remarks.[18] Modest dress encourages respect from those who tend to emphasize physical appearance, she feels. This offers a sort of freedom many intelligent, independent women appreciate.

Many modern young Muslim women also wear the hijab or other coverings with pride and a sense of identity. Some choose it against the preferences of parents who have adopted Western clothing. Professor of Islam Yvonne Haddad, referencing the hijab, explains, "The little scarf is saying, 'I am Muslim, and I have a presence here.'"[19] For others, often just as devout, it becomes a burden. When those outside of Islam question or criticize the religion, they often direct their comments toward

Some Muslim women wear coverings not because it is required but because it represents what they believe in.

women who cover. "I was tired of being a political spokesperson for my faith," says attorney Asma Uddin, a Pakistani American. "I was tired of trying to prove that Muslim women in headscarves are also empowered."[20]

Covering can make it difficult to befriend non-Muslims. When Westerners see a woman in covering, they avoid interacting with her, never taking the opportunity to test their assumptions about Islam. After 9/11, some Muslim women in the United States, identified by their attire, were subject to discrimination and harassment. Some were even attacked, on occasion fatally. Other Westerners see these coverings as symbols of oppression and wish the women could be freed from them. France led Europe in outlawing face coverings in 2011. French president Nicolas Sarkozy argued that veils oppress women. In 2017, Canada's Quebec province made most face coverings illegal in public places such as on buses. Supporters cited public safety reasons, saying faces are important for identifying a person. But only 3 percent of Canada's Muslim women wore niqabs at the time the law passed. "It seems like a made-up solution to an invented problem," said Ihsaan Gardee of the National Council of Canadian Muslims.[21] Gardee noted that there aren't any real problems with these women in public. For women who are used to and choose this covering, appearing in public without it may feel like walking through town in a bathing suit. Some critics argue that the government shouldn't pass clothing laws, especially as other religious clothing, such as Jewish caps, called yarmulke, are not restricted.

Amid the debates, many Muslims hold to Muhammad's example. He raised women's position and set an example of kindness and partnership. He accepted a woman's right to earn a living. His pride in and praise of his daughter Fatimah also signaled the value of women and daughters. Islamic studies professor Akbar S. Ahmed points out that Muslim women have a right to education and professional achievement. The Koran upholds various rights for women: they can initiate divorce, inherit property, and write a will, all advantages they did not have previously and that were not granted to many Western women until the 1900s.

ISLAM TODAY AND INTO THE FUTURE

Muslims are a growing and diverse part of the United States. They number approximately 3.45 million, more than one-half having immigrated from different nations. The largest group comes from South Asia, especially Pakistan. By birth or naturalization, which is the process of becoming a citizen, 82 percent of these Muslim immigrants are American citizens.[1]

Most immigrants must make many changes on moving to a new country. The new country often has a different history, language, monetary system, and more. New cultural practices can be unsettling. Having beliefs that are different from the majority can further hinder the feeling of fitting in. When ignorance,

The Islamic Center of America in Dearborn, Michigan, serves both as a place of worship and a place to teach others about Islam.

misunderstanding, and negative media portrayals are added, as they often are for Muslims in Western nations, it becomes even more difficult to settle in.

College student Hussain Tariq describes how stereotypes can alienate Muslim Americans: "I was walking through the metal detectors at the building I worked in. Meanwhile, the security guard was looking through my bag and asked, 'No weapons of mass destruction today?' I did not know how to answer her. Out of complete shock, I just collected my belongings and walked away."[2]

Some such remarks are meant as jokes, thoughtless as they may be. But repeated occurrences, coupled with suspicious or fearful looks and other slights, add to the feeling of isolation. And the problem goes deeper than assaults on a person's sense of belonging. Fourteen-year-old Ahmed Mohamed of Texas constructed a working clock. Proud of his success,

AMERICA'S ATTITUDES TOWARD MUSLIMS

In 2014, the Pew Research Center asked Americans how they felt about Muslims. Recording results as if on a thermometer, with 100 points the warmest possible feelings and 0 the coldest, Americans registered just 40 degrees.[3]

The 2017 results offered some improvement, though Muslims remained below every other religious group. Jews, with 67, and Catholics, 66, are at the top. Then the list drifts downward from mainstream Protestants, evangelical Christians, Buddhists, Hindus, and Mormons to atheists at 50 degrees and Muslims coming in last at 48.[4]

he took it to his school to show his teacher. Instead of admiring his work, she said it looked like a bomb. Because she simply set it on her desk, some argue she knew it was not a bomb. But Ahmed was removed from class and questioned by five police officers and two school administrators.

In 2017, nearly one-half of Muslim Americans said they had recently been the target of religious discrimination, according to the Pew Research Center. This parallels the negative feelings Americans report toward Muslims. Those feelings, though, have improved some over the years. Some Muslim Americans say that they've felt supported as Muslims recently, with 55 percent calling Americans usually "friendly" toward them.[5] However, a large majority of Muslim Americans—and especially Muslim women—worry about President Donald Trump's policies targeting them. Muslims and non-Muslims alike recognize that Muslims face much discrimination and unfair media coverage.

As in the United States, the growth of Islam in Europe is largely due to immigration. Studies indicate Europe's population will be

A DISCRIMINATION SCALE

Discrimination is hard to measure. In 2017, the Pew Research Center reported that 75 percent of Muslims in the United States said they deal with "a lot of discrimination."[6] Sixty-nine percent of non-Muslim Americans agreed that Muslims face more discrimination than other minority groups. In comparison, 59 percent of non-Muslims said black people face a great deal of discrimination, 58 percent said gays and lesbians face such discrimination, and 56 percent said Hispanics face such discrimination.[7]

COUNTRIES WITH THE MOST MUSLIMS IN 2010[8]

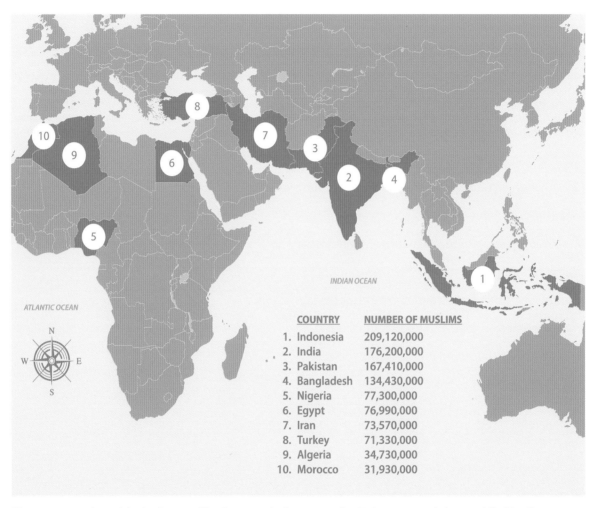

COUNTRY	NUMBER OF MUSLIMS
1. Indonesia	209,120,000
2. India	176,200,000
3. Pakistan	167,410,000
4. Bangladesh	134,430,000
5. Nigeria	77,300,000
6. Egypt	76,990,000
7. Iran	73,570,000
8. Turkey	71,330,000
9. Algeria	34,730,000
10. Morocco	31,930,000

INDIAN OCEAN

ATLANTIC OCEAN

The ten countries with the largest Muslim populations contain 65.8 percent of the world's Muslims.

8 percent Muslim by 2030 if trends continue. Eastern and southern Europeans tend to distrust and disapprove of Muslims, while attitudes in western and northern Europe are more positive.[9] Fifty-five percent of 10,000 Europeans surveyed in 2017 favored halting immigration from Muslim-majority nations.[10] Researchers noted that younger people and college graduates tended to be more open to Muslim immigrants.

Only 55 percent of non-Muslim Americans know a Muslim.[11] Those who do tend to view the religion and its followers more favorably than those who do not. Lack of knowledge fuels fear and suspicion; with knowledge comes understanding and less fear and ill feelings.

Muslims in the West aren't the only ones facing discrimination. More than 688,000 Muslims fled Burma between August 2017 and January 2018.[12] The Burmese government and Buddhists have plundered Muslim homes and killed thousands of Muslims.

Feminism and Islam

Around the world, Muslims are trying to define what position Islam prescribes for women. A study published by the American Psychological Association in 2008 showed that most practicing Muslim women in the United States called themselves feminists and believed their religion supports feminism. Indeed, many Muslim women have risen to prominence for their achievements in diverse fields in modern times. For example, two women, Asmahan Youssef al-Wihidi and Khulud Mohamed Ahmed Faqih, passed their exams and were appointed judges in Palestine in 2009. Both were former

Ibtihaj Muhammad celebrated her Olympic bronze medal on the podium.

THE INTERNATIONAL MUSLIM FEMINIST MOVEMENT

A 12-member body of Muslim women from various nations, including Egypt, Gambia, Turkey, and Pakistan, started Musawah, or "equality," in 2009. The aim of the Malaysia-based organization is to show women that they can both be faithful Muslims and champion equal rights and justice. Promoting a feminist interpretation of the Koran, the group encourages members to work for changes in laws and customs in their homelands.

Musawah was inspired by the Malaysian group Sisters in Islam (Sisters), cofounded by Amina Wadud, an African American feminist professor who converted to Islam when she was 20. Organized in 1988, Sisters tackled oppression in Malaysia by working with Islamic scholars to create workshops showing that Islam upholds women's rights. Sisters founder and Musawah cofounder Zainah Anwar laments, "All these years, they believed that their suffering in the form of abandonment, polygamy and beatings was all in the name of God." Sisters has seen the culture shifting since its founding. Increasingly, women armed with evidence from the Koran confront husbands who mistreat them. When the appeal is to God's law, they say, husbands respond more readily. "Women are claiming the authority to speak on Islamic law," Anwar notes. "Musawah's ambition is to multiply and amplify this voice at an international level."[13]

lawyers. Khulud often defended women's rights in particular. Pakistani Sharmeen Obaid-Chinoy is a filmmaker and journalist whose work often explores the unequal treatment of women. *Time* magazine recognized her as one of the world's 100 most influential people in 2012. An American Muslim, Ibtihaj Muhammad, won a bronze medal in the 2016 Olympics for fencing. In 2017, Mattel introduced "Hijabi Barbie," modeled after her.

EARLY MUSLIM CONTRIBUTORS

Muslims have made many contributions to the world. The ancient Greeks thought human eyes released light rays. But after creating the first pinhole camera in the 900s, Ibn al-Haitham, a mathematician, astronomer, and physicist, made a discovery. Human eyes receive light as his camera did.

Mariam al-'Ijliya helped introduce astrolabes to the Islamic world in the 900s CE. The astrolabe, a device for computing the positions of the sun and planets, was an early version of a computer that goes back to the early Greeks. Her work improved the devices, and even her city's ruler recognized her contributions.

Al-Jazari created the crankshaft along with other inventions detailed in his *Book of Knowledge of Ingenious Mechanical Devices*, published in 1206. Today, most machines require a crankshaft, a device that turns circular motion into forward (and backward) motion. A simple example is a bicycle, where pushing the pedals turns its wheels. Al-Jazari is considered the father of modern engineering and robotics.

Muslims used astrolabes to determine the direction toward Mecca.

Al-Zahrawi was an innovative surgeon. This doctor from the 900s also invented 200 surgical instruments, many of them very similar to those used today.[14] He also created internal stitches that naturally dissolved.

PERSPECTIVES

WHO IS MALALA?

When a Taliban gunman boarded a Pakistani school bus in 2012 and shot Malala Yousafzai in the face, no one could predict that the 15-year-old would impact the world—or even that she would live. Of that moment, Malala would later say, "My weaknesses died on that day."[15] She had been targeted for continuing her education beyond the age of nine. The Taliban forbade education for girls beyond that age. Through an anonymous blog, she encouraged others to do so as well.

Malala recovered and, from her new home in the United Kingdom, found that her voice speaking out for girls' education had a global reach. She helped establish a charity that had devoted $8.4 million to the cause as of January 2017.[16] At 16, she addressed the United Nations. In 2014, at age 17, she became the youngest winner of the Nobel Peace Prize. In 2017, she became a student at the University of Oxford in England.

Muslim feminists around the world—female and male—state that the Prophet Muhammad promoted gender equality. The problem, they say, has been male-only interpreters of the Koran. They feel that when people share their diverse interpretations, the Koran's true intention is better understood. Islamic feminists recall stories of Muhammad's dealings with women and many advances he brought, such as the rights to inherit, divorce, and reject a proposed marriage. How feminist Islam truly is depends on the cultural circumstances in a particular place and time, along with the ways in which followers choose to interpret the religion.

Evolving Islam

When cultures meet, things change. Ideas are shared and shaped. People often feel torn. They want to feel they're being true to their roots, and yet they may be attracted to new ideas. As do followers of all faiths, Muslims wrestle with the lure of material things. Science brings up new moral issues, such as fertility procedures, cloning, and artificially prolonging or ending life, that religions' original teachings could not address. New historical research methods question certain texts' authorship, interpretations, and translations, particularly the hadiths. And some Muslims ask whether laws and penalties formed around earlier societies' customs by earlier scholars are suitable today.

Contact with other people and ideas offers opportunities for growth. Again, like people of other religions, Muslims take varied positions. Some Muslims believe Islam should touch every part of life, and others believe in the Western notion of separation of religion and state. Some believe laws should match those in Muhammad's time, while others feel the Koran allows for new interpretations and adjustments to meet evolving needs and circumstances. Some feel a wholly Islamic society is ideal, while others celebrate the diversity of many Western nations. How Islam comes to terms with such issues will help determine its future.

As Ahmed states in *Islam Today,* "The globe has shrunk." Nations are connected through economics, finances, transportation, and communication. Most people understand that people's fates are linked. Ahmed concludes, "It is time for the people of vision to transcend their positions and aim to build bridges toward each other into the next millennium."[17]

ESSENTIAL FACTS

DATE FOUNDED

Islam began with Muhammad's first revelation in 610 CE in Mecca.

BASIC BELIEFS

Islam is based on the belief in the same God described in Judaism and Christianity. He is referred to as Allah, the Arabic word for "God." Muslims believe Muhammad is the final prophet from God, and that all believers, regardless of race or nationality, are equal before God.

IMPORTANT HOLIDAYS AND EVENTS

- Eid al-Adha, the Festivity of Sacrifice, commemorating Abraham's willingness to sacrifice his son to God
- Eid al-Fitr, the Festivity of Breaking the Fast

FAITH LEADERS

- Farid Esack has often been called upon to answer questions about his faith.
- Imam Kamil Mufti has training in Islamic law and an education in Western science.
- Muhammad was the prophet to whom God made his final revelation.

NUMBER OF PEOPLE WHO PRACTICE ISLAM

Islam is a fast-growing religion and the second largest, with approximately 1.8 billion Muslims around the world.

QUOTE

"Muslim women do have their own struggles among their Muslim brethren and have to fight for their rights, this is no different than Western women fighting for their rights of equal pay and freedom from sexual harassment. Even within Sharia, women are arguing that certain things need to change and they are becoming Islamic law jurists and judges."

— Sana Tayyen, visiting scholar and professor at the University of Southern California and the University of Redlands

GLOSSARY

CALLIGRAPHY
Artistic handwriting.

CIVIC
Having to do with being a citizen.

DEHUMANIZE
To treat someone as though he or she is not a human being.

FAST
A period of time during which a person does not eat at all or does not eat specific foods.

FUNDAMENTALISM
A form of a religion that follows a strict interpretation of the religion's texts and laws.

HAREM
A group of women who are the wives or female relatives of the wives of one man.

HOMAGE
Something that is done to honor someone or something.

ILLITERATE
Unable to read or write.

IMPERIALISM
A policy in which a country attempts to increase its power through military force and by controlling colonies in other parts of the world.

INFALLIBLE
Free from error.

METEORITE
A solid piece of debris from a meteoroid that comes from outer space through the Earth's atmosphere and lands on its surface.

MOSQUE
An Islamic place of worship.

NOMAD

A person who travels from place to place with no fixed home.

OASIS

A fertile area in the desert where there is water.

OBJECTIFY

To treat as an object, a thing.

OMNISCIENT

All knowing.

PILGRIMAGE

A long journey to a sacred place to show devotion.

PROSTRATE

To stretch out with one's face to the ground in submission.

PUBERTY

The beginning of physical maturity when a person becomes capable of reproducing sexually.

REPENT

To feel sorrow about one's sins, try to quit sinning, and live a right life.

RITE

A ceremonial practice.

SECT

A group within a larger religion that holds distinct beliefs from others in that religion.

TERRORISM

The illegal use of violence and intimidation against unarmed civilians, usually to accomplish a political goal.

UNWIELDY

Cumbersome, not easy to manage.

ADDITIONAL RESOURCES

SELECTED BIBLIOGRAPHY

Esposito, John L., Darrell J. Fasching, and Todd Lewis. *World Religions Today*. New York: Oxford UP, 2002. Print.

Fisher, Mary Pat. *Living Religions*. Upper Saddle River, NJ: Prentice-Hall, 1999. Print.

Haleem, M. A. S. Abdel. *The Qur'an*. New York: Oxford UP, 2005. Print.

Momen, Moojan. *An Introduction to Shi'i Islam: The History and Doctrines of Twelver Shi'ism*. New Haven, CT: Yale UP, 1985. Print.

FURTHER READINGS

Kenney, Karen Latchana. *Iran*. Minneapolis: Abdo, 2012.

1001 Inventions & Awesome Facts from Muslim Civilization. Washington, DC: National Geographic, 2012. Print.

Rowell, Rebecca. *Malala Yousafzai: Education Activist*. Minneapolis: Abdo, 2014.

ONLINE RESOURCES

To learn more about Islam, visit **abdobooklinks.com**. These links are routinely monitored and updated to provide the most current information available.

MORE INFORMATION

For more information on this subject, contact or visit the following organizations:

COUNCIL ON AMERICAN ISLAMIC RELATIONS (CAIR)

453 New Jersey Ave. SE
Washington, DC 20003
202-488-8787
cair.com

CAIR promotes justice and understanding for Muslim Americans by fighting stereotypes, encouraging dialogue, and protecting civil liberties. It has chapters in cities throughout the nation.

GAINPEACE

1S270 Summit Ave., Suite 204
Oakbrook Terrace, IL 60181
800-662-47526
gainpeace.com

GainPeace is a source of information about Islam for the general public and for new Muslims.

SOURCE NOTES

Chapter 1. Fasting and Feasting

1. "Ramadan for Kids." *Time Out Dubai*. ITP Digital Media, 26 July 2011. Web. 27 Mar. 2018.

2. Greg Mellen. "20,000 Muslims Gather at Eid Prayer Celebration in Anaheim." *Orange County Register*. Southern California News Group, 25 June 2017. Web. 27 Mar. 2018.

3. Mellen, "20,000 Muslims Gather."

4. John L. Esposito. "The Five Pillars of Islam." *Islam: The Straight Path*. Oxford University Press USA, n.d. Web. 27 Mar. 2018.

5. "Eid al-Fitr 2107: Everything You Need to Know." *Al Jazeera*. Al Jazeera, 20 June 2017. Web. 27 Mar. 2018.

6. "Let Them Eat Cake." *Washington Report on Middle East Affairs* 25.9 (Dec. 2006). *Academic Search Complete*. Web. 27 Mar. 2018.

Chapter 2. The Prophet Muhammad

1. Walter H. Wagner. *Opening the Qur'an: Introducing Islam's Holy Book*. Notre Dame, IN: University of Notre Dame, 2008. *Google Books*. Web. 28 Mar. 2018.

2. Abdullah Yusuf Ali, trans. *The Holy Qur'ān: Text, Translation & Commentary*. New Revised ed. Brentwood, MD: Amana, 1989. Print. Sura 96:1–5.

3. "Night Journey." *Oxford Islamic Studies Online*. Oxford UP, 2018. Web. 28 Mar. 2018.

4. Mary Pat Fisher. *Living Religions*. 4th ed. Upper Saddle River, NJ: Prentice-Hall, 1999. Print. 351.

5. Akbar S. Ahmed. *Islam Today: A Short Introduction to the Muslim World*. New York: I. B. Tauris, 2008. Print. 155.

6. Ahmed, *Islam Today*, 20.

7. Fisher, *Living Religions*, 337.

Chapter 3. The Years after the Prophet

1. Moojan Momen. *An Introduction to Shi'i Islam: The History and Doctrines of Twelver Shi'ism*. New Haven: Yale UP, 1985. Print. 12.

2. Momen, *An Introduction to Shi'i Islam*, 15.

3. "Islam Fast Facts." *CNN*. CNN, 21 Sept. 2017. Web. 28 Mar. 2018.

4. Fergus M. Bordewich. "A Flourishing of Whirling Dervishes." *New York Times*. New York Times, 1987. Web. 28 Mar. 2018.

5. Barbara H. Rosenwein. *A Short History of the Middle Ages, Volume I: From c.300 to c.1150*. 4th ed. Ontario: U of Toronto, 2014. *Google Books*. 125. Web. 28 Mar. 2018.

6. Margaret Smith. *Rabi'a: The Life & Work of Rabi'a and Other Women Mystics in Islam*. Oxford: Oneworld, 1994. Print. 31.

7. John L. Esposito, Darrell J. Fasching, and Todd Lewis. *World Religions Today*. New York: Oxford UP, 2002. Print. 224–225.

8. Esposito, Fasching, and Lewis, *World Religions Today*, 228–229.

Chapter 4. Core Beliefs

1. Abdullah Yusuf Ali, trans. *The Holy Qur'ān: Text, Translation & Commentary*. New Revised ed. Brentwood, MD: Amana, 1989. Print. Sura 29:46.

2. "John 14:26: New International Version (NIV)." *BibleGateway*. Bible Gateway, n.d. Web. 28 Mar. 2018.

3. Ali, *The Holy Qur'ān*, sura 33:40.

4. Ali, *The Holy Qur'ān*, sura 55:33.

5. Kamil Mufti. "Belief in Divine Decree." *Religion of Islam*. IslamReligion.com, 4 Jan. 2015. Web. 28 Mar. 2018.

Chapter 5. The Practice of Islam

1. Sana Tayyen, email message to editor, 24 Jan. 2018.

2. John L. Esposito, Darrell J. Fasching, and Todd Lewis. *World Religions Today*. New York: Oxford UP, 2002. Print. 194, 206.

3. "Shahadah: The Statement of Faith." *BBC Religions*. BBC, 28 Aug. 2009. Web. 28 Mar. 2018.

4. Esposito, Fasching, and Lewis, *World Religions Today*, 210.

5. Esposito, Fasching, and Lewis, *World Religions Today*, 212.

6. Abdullah Yusuf Ali, trans. *The Holy Qur'ān: Text, Translation & Commentary*. New Revised ed. Brentwood, MD: Amana, 1989. Print. Sura 22:39.

7. Rubaina Azhar. "For an American Pilgrim in Saudi Arabia, a Discovery of Fellowship." *Los Angeles Times*. Los Angeles Times, 5 Nov. 2011. Web. 28 Mar. 2018.

8. Azhar, "For an American Pilgrim in Saudi Arabia."

9. Ali, *The Holy Qur'ān*, suras 2:192–193.

10. Mary Pat Fisher. *Religions Today: An Introduction*. Abingdon, UK: Routledge, 2002. *Google Books*. 231. Web. 28 Mar. 2018. 244.

11. Fisher. *Religions Today: An Introduction*, 231.

12. Roger S. Gottlieb, ed. *Liberating Faith: Religious Voices for Justice, Peace, and Ecological Wisdom*. Lanham, MD: Rowman & Littlefield, 2003. *Google Books*. 136. Web. 28 Mar. 2018.

Chapter 6. East Meets West

1. John L. Esposito, Darrell J. Fasching, and Todd Lewis. *World Religions Today*. New York: Oxford UP, 2002. Print. 255.

2. Abdullah Yusuf Ali, trans. *The Holy Qur'ān: Text, Translation & Commentary*. New Revised ed. Brentwood, MD: Amana, 1989. Print. Sura 30:22.

3. "The Last Sermon of Prophet Muhammad." *Arab News: Islam in Perspective*. Saudi Research & Publishing Company, 11 Oct. 2013. Web. 28 Mar. 2018.

4. "1993 World Trade Center Bombing Fast Facts." *CNN*. CNN, 28 Feb. 2018. Web. 28 Mar. 2018.

5. Samra Habib. "Islamophobia Is on the Rise in the US. But So Is Islam." *PRI's The World*. PRI, 9 Sept. 2016. Web. 28 Mar. 2018.

6. "US Muslims Concerned About Their Place in Society, but Continue to Believe in the American Dream: 5. Terrorism and Concerns about Extremism." *Pew Research Center*. Pew Research Center, 26 July 2017. Web. 28 Mar. 2018.

7. "In Nations with Significant Muslim Populations, Much Disdain for ISIS." *FactTank*. Pew Research Center, 17 Nov. 2015. Web. 28 Mar. 2018.

8. Ruth Alexander and Hannah Moore. "Are Most Victims of Terrorism Muslim?" *BBC News Magazine*. BBC, 20 Jan. 2015. Web. 28 Mar. 2018.

SOURCE NOTES CONTINUED

Chapter 7. Debates and Misconceptions

1. Belinda Espiritu. "Islamophobia and Negative Media Portrayal of Islam." *Media Development* 63.1 (Feb. 2016): 4. *ResearchGate*. Web. 28 Mar. 2018.

2. Saifuddin Ahmed and Jörg Matthes. "Media Representation of Muslims and Islam from 2000 to 2015: A Meta-Analysis." *ResearchGate*. ResearchGate, Apr. 2017. Web. 28 Mar. 2018.

3. "'Sorry That Freedom of Religion Offended': Quebec Zoo Fends Off Criticism for Allowing Muslim Prayers." *CBC*. CBC/Radio-Canada, 5 July 2017. Web. 28 Mar. 2018.

4. Jack G. Shaheen. "Reel Bad Arabs: How Hollywood Vilifies a People." *Annals of the American Academy of Political and Social Science*. American Academy of Political & Social Science, 1 July 2003. Web. 28 Mar. 2018.

5. Jack G. Shaheen. "Hollywood's Muslim Arabs." *Muslim World* 90.1–2 (Spring 2000): 22–42. *Hartford Seminary*. Web. 28 Mar. 2018.

6. Shaheen, "Hollywood's Muslim Arabs."

7. Rubina Ramji. "Examining the Critical Role American Popular Film Continues to Play in Maintaining the Muslim Terrorist Image, Post 9/11." *Journal of Religion and Film* 20.1 (4 Jan. 2016). *Academic OneFile*. Web. 28 Mar. 2018.

8. Akbar S. Ahmed. *Islam Today: A Short Introduction to the Muslim World*. New York: I. B. Tauris, 2008. Print. 19.

9. Abdullah Yusuf Ali, trans. *The Holy Qur'ān: Text, Translation & Commentary*. New Revised ed. Brentwood, MD: Amana, 1989. Print. Sura 4:3.

10. Ali, *The Holy Qur'ān*, sura 4:129.

11. Dan Cohn-Sherbok, George D. Chryssides, and Dawoud El-Alami. *Love, Sex and Marriage: Insights from Judaism, Christianity and Islam*. London: SCM, 2013. *Google Books*. 120. Web. 28 Mar. 2018.

12. Ahmed, *Islam Today*, 152.

13. Ziauddin Sardar. "Forced Marriages Disgrace Islam." *New Statesman*. New Statesman, 27 Mar. 2008. Web. 28 Mar. 2018.

14. Hiba Masood. "A Tale of Two Marriages: Aliyah Furqan's Story." *Islamic Horizons* 39.6 (3 Oct. 2010): 32–34. *ISSUU*. Web. 28 Mar. 2018.

15. Laleh Bakhtiar. "The Sublime Quran: The Misinterpretation of Chapter 4 Verse 34." *European Journal of Women's Studies* 18.4 (1 Oct. 2006): 431–439. *Academic Search Complete*. Web. 1 Oct. 2017.

16. Bakhtiar, "The Sublime Quran."

17. Ali, *The Holy Qur'ān*, sura 24:31.

18. Soraya Salam. "Muslim Women Who Wear the Hijab and Niqab Explain Their Choice." *Belief Blog*. CNN, 23 Aug. 2010. Web. 28 Mar. 2018.

19. Salam, "Muslim Women Who Wear the Hijab and Niqab."

20. Tom Gjelten. "American Muslim Women Explain Why They Do—or Don't—Cover." *Code Switch*. NPR, 2 Feb. 2016. Web. 28 Mar. 2018.

21. Ashifa Kassam. "Quebec Passes Law Banning Facial Coverings in Public." *Guardian*. Guardian, 18 Oct. 2017. Web. 28 Mar. 2018.

Chapter 8. Islam Today and Into the Future

1. "US Muslims Concerned about Their Place in Society, but Continue to Believe in the American Dream." *Pew Research Center: Religion and Public Life*. Pew Research Center, 26 July 2017. Web. 28 Mar. 2018.

2. Briana Williams. "Islamaphobia through the Eyes of Muslim Students at U of L." *Louisville Cardinal*. Louisville Cardinal, 8 Jan. 2017. Web. 28 Mar. 2018.

3. "US Muslims Concerned about Their Place in Society, but Continue to Believe in the American Dream: 7. How the US General Public Views Muslims and Islam." *Pew Research Center*. Pew Research Center, 26 July 2017. Web. 28 Mar. 2018.

4. "7. How the US General Public Views Muslims and Islam."

5. "US Muslims Concerned about their Place in Society."

6. "US Muslims Concerned about their Place in Society."

7. "7. How the US General Public Views Muslims and Islam."

8. "10 Countries with the Largest Muslim Populations, 2010 and 2050." *Pew Research Center: Religion & Public Life*. Pew Research Center, 2 Apr. 2015. Web. 28 Mar. 2018.

9. Conrad Hackett. "5 Facts about the Muslim Population in Europe." *FactTank*. Pew Research Center. 19 July 2016. Web. 28 Mar. 2018.

10. David Reid. "Europe's Fear of Muslim Immigration Revealed in Widespread Survey." *CNBC*. CBNC, 8 Feb. 2017. Web. 28 Mar. 2018.

11. "7. How the US General Public Views Muslims and Islam."

12. Scott Neuman. "AP Investigation Details Shocking Massacre, Mass Graves of Myanmar Rohingya." *The Two-Way*. NPR, 1 Feb. 2018. Web. 28 Mar. 2018.

13. Elizabeth Segran. "The Rise of the Islamic Feminists." *Nation*. Nation, 4 Dec. 2013. Web. 28 Mar. 2018.

14. "How Islamic Inventors Changed the World." *Independent*. Independent, 11 Mar. 2006. Web. 28 Mar. 2018.

15. Kerry A. Dolan. "Nobel Peace Prize Winner Malala on Being Shot: 'My Weaknesses Died on that Day.'" *Forbes*. Forbes, 1 Dec. 2014. Web. 28 Mar. 2018.

16. Mirren Gidda. "Malala Yousafzai's New Mission: Can She Still Inspire as an Adult?" *Newsweek*. Newsweek, 11 Jan. 2017. Web. 28 Mar. 2018.

17. Akbar S. Ahmed. *Islam Today: A Short Introduction to the Muslim World*. New York: I. B. Tauris, 2008. Print. 230–231.

INDEX

ABOUT THE AUTHOR

Gail Radley, a freelance writer, recently contributed to the book *Sexism at Work* for Abdo's Being Female in America set. She lives and works in DeLand, Florida, where she also teaches English at Stetson University.